On Moving

A Writer's Meditation on New Houses,
Old Haunts, and Finding Home Again

Louise DeSalvo

B L O O M S B U R Y

NEW YORK BERLIN LONDON

Published by Bloomsbury USA, New York

All papers used by Bloomsbury USA are natural, recyclable products made from
wood grown in well-managed forests. The manufacturing processes conform to the
environmental regulations of the country of origin.

Quotations from Elizabeth Bishop's poems are taken from Elizabeth Bishop, *The
Complete Poems: 1927–1979* (New York: Farrar, Straus and Giroux, 1983).

LIBRARY OF CONGRESS CATALOGING-IN-PUBLICATION DATA

DeSalvo, Louise A., 1942–
On moving : a writer's meditation on new houses, old haunts, and finding home again /
Louise DeSalvo.—1st U.S. ed.
p. cm.
ISBN-13: 978-1-58234-581-9
ISBN-10: 1-58234-581-3
1. DeSalvo, Louise A., 1942– —Homes and haunts. 2. Critics—United
States—Biography. 3. Home—Psychological aspects. 4. Dwellings—Psychological
aspects. 5. Home in literature. 6. Dwellings in literature. 7. Authors, English—
Homes and haunts. 8. Authors, American—Homes and haunts. I. Title.

PR55.D47A3 2009
809—dc22
[B]
2008040977

First U.S. Edition 2009

1 3 5 7 9 10 8 6 4 2

Designed by Sara Stemen
Typeset by Westchester Book Group
Printed in the United States of America by Quebecor World Fairfield

for Geri Thoma, for Julia Galbus,
for Christina Baker Kline, for Pamela Satran,
in memory of my parents and my grandparents,
for my family,
and for Ernie, as ever, who has made every house a home

How easy it was to long for a different life,
how hard it was to find one's way there.
EVA HOFFMAN, *Lost in Translation: A Life in a New Language*

The great affair is to move; to feel the needs
and hitches of life a little more nearly.
RICHARD HOLMES, *Footsteps*

Comes over one an absolute necessity to move. And what
is more, to move in some particular direction. A double
necessity then: to get on the move, and to know whither.
D. H. LAWRENCE, *The Sea and Sardinia*

The hard part is the moving, but maybe staying can be harder.
CONSTANCE FENIMORE WOOLSON TO HENRY JAMES,
IN COLM TÓIBÍN, *The Master*

Contents

Introduction

When, in the autumn of 2003, my husband, Ernie, and I move for the first time in more than thirty years, my thoughts and emotions become unsettled. I'd looked forward to this move. Yet I was experiencing a sense of loss almost as profound as when my mother died a few years before. Surely a move shouldn't feel like mourning the passing of a family member. But it did.

I sought to learn from friends and acquaintances whether their moves too had unleashed such a storm of feelings. I wanted their wise counsel, their solace. But mostly I wanted to hear that I wasn't the only one who felt this way, that others also believed their lives had been torn apart. I wanted to learn how they became accustomed to a new place—what they did to temper the trauma of a move.

I contacted friends who'd moved recently, some across the country, some across an ocean. One said, "I'd rather not talk about it"; another, "It was awful but you'll get over it"; a third, "What can I say? It's best endured and forgotten, the sooner the better"; still another said, "It took me a year to scrub the old inhabitants out of my house." Only one person immediately felt excited and energized by moving and leaving her old life, embracing her new life without regret. Beyond these glimmers of their responses to moving, I learned nothing. Is moving so difficult that once it's past people want to forget the whole experience? Is moving such a significant part of the American dream that discussing the often difficult reality of this experience is taboo? But even if we don't talk about it, feel the pain we do. I myself discovered moving entails significant emotional and physical consequences. It ranks as the third-most-stressful life experience (after the death of a spouse and the loss of a job). If a move involves losing a cherished home, or if a move is desired but cannot be undertaken because of financial issues, normal stresses are, of course, greatly magnified.

This book began as an attempt to examine my thoughts and feelings about moving. But it developed to include how a score of other writers and thinkers have written about the subject. It seems that the written word is far better than conversation for describing the reality of this complex transition. I wrote this book to record the most useful moving histories I found, those that aided me in understanding my own experience in the context of my family's and my past; I hope that it will help readers gain a new perspective on this, one of our most significant life experiences, and that it will impel them to reconstruct the history of this important transition in their own lives.

I began by keeping a journal. But because I wanted this to be more than a personal story, I quickly moved to reading the letters, journals, memoirs, poetry, and fiction of my favorite writers and other creative people, searching for what they said about the experience of moving as it was occurring and their reflections on it years after. I wondered whether they would be extremely conscious of the effect of moving upon their lives and work.

Did Virginia Woolf reflect on her moves? Did as lofty a thinker as Sigmund Freud care about where he lived, how he furnished his home? What about Carl Jung, preoccupied by pondering the mythic dimensions of everyday life? Or Pierre Bonnard, that divine painter of interior spaces? Or D. H. Lawrence, driven from England by the censorship of his work and his expulsion from Cornwall? Or the Pulitzer Prize–winning poet Elizabeth Bishop, who moved often and to far-flung places? Or Henry Miller, who left New York for Paris nearly penniless—did he plumb this transition's meanings?

As I worked, I learned that these figures indeed reflected on their moves and the significance of their new homes; they often compared a recent move with one past, a new home with one lost to them; they often thought about these moves in the context of their early lives, trying to discover how their family history impacted their choices of domiciles as adults, trying to find a pattern in their experiences that would render them more meaningful. Sometimes their later thoughts about a move are quite different from how they first assess it. It seems that moves can develop a mythic quality as they recede into the past and that the meanings we assign them help us define who we were, who we've become, and what remains: a person who needs stability; one who's a wanderer and profits from a frequent change of scene; one who needs to be rooted in the past. Sometimes, though, these creative people reflected on the fact that what they seemed to need was faulty and that acting on the basis of these suppositions harmed them.

I was astonished by how much detailed information they recorded about their moves—their dream houses, their search for the right home, their decorating schemes, the changes in their lives and work as a result of their moves—how illuminating their insights invariably were, and how much they helped me understand my own move and the history of my family's. I learned that these people, often presumed not to be overly concerned with household matters, were invariably passionate about domestic architecture and interior decoration. And many codified a personal philosophy or mythology about moving—what it signified, how it related to their past histories, how it affected their lives and work, its universal meaning. Those who simply moved without reflecting on its impact or realistically assessing their needs did so at their peril.

I learned that there can be significant creative payoffs to well-chosen or lucky moves. The way we construct the world, see ourselves, and do our work can shift because of them. I learned that the psychic cost of moving, even of a good move, can be considerable, for it seems that each move reawakens other losses we've experienced. I learned that our moves often recall those of our ancestors, even those whose moving histories are unknown to us, for the significance of what moving meant to our forebears seems to be transmuted through the generations, sometimes nonverbally. It became clear that families often define themselves in terms of the moves they or their forebears have made, and this sometimes burdens the younger members, who are expected to repair difficult relocations by behaving in proscribed ways and who are pressured to look back rather than to the future; that some of us move because we think that moving alone will change us and that some of us move because we think finding the perfect place to live will erase all sorrow; that people sometimes try to make unfamiliar places feel like a home they've left to adjust to the transition; and that it's tragic to yearn for a place that feels like home yet never find it, although this never-ending quest can yield its own rewards.

So many people in the United States move—the typical American moves 11.7 times in a lifetime; that's forty-two million people or 25 percent of all adults in a single year. On average, homeowners will sell the house they live in and move every five to seven years (living more than thirty years in one home, like I have done, is unusual).

These statistics indicate that each year one in four adults in the United States undergo the stress and psychic and physical effects of moving like those described by the writers and thinkers whose lives I've studied. Yet few of us psychically prepare ourselves for a move—I didn't—even as many of us prepare ourselves for other significant shifts in our lives, for example, the birth of a child. So many of us are blindsided by moving's almost inevitable consequences, as I was.

People who are relocating spend more money in the three months before and after a move than others spend in five years, so the stress of moving is often compounded by financial worries, especially during times of economic hardship, and especially if it makes us "house poor." By learning about others' experiences with moving, understanding its complexity, and making wiser choices, I believe we can significantly alter our experience for the better.

When people are forced to relocate because of natural disaster or human tragedy, there is often a groundswell of support for those affected—at least temporarily. But sometimes people forced to move are greeted with hostility and persecution—those trying to penetrate closed borders because work is impossible to find in their homelands, for example. And people choosing to move or having to move because a job necessitates it rarely get emotional support; their moves are regarded as advantageous, not hardships, thus not meriting sympathy and sometimes even eliciting feelings of envy. Most people who move don't talk about the difficulty of their experiences, as I learned, or don't believe they have the right to feel unsettled. After all, isn't moving to a better place, making a fresh start, beginning a new life, part of the American dream, something to be grateful for and not complain about?

Perhaps many of us living in the United States are so transient because we are descended from those who've come from afar, hoping for a better life. But whether our restlessness is part of our psychic makeup, necessitated by complex economic forces, or learned behavior, who can say. Perhaps we repeat family history and move because in so doing we hope that it will reward us with a better life. For those of us choosing to move, the idea that somewhere there is "a domestic Eden"—D. H. Lawrence's term for the place where you'll finally feel at home, where your spirit will find peace and your life will blossom—seems to be deeply ingrained in our collective imagination. When we find this place, we imagine we'll have everything we need to nourish the human spirit.

This kind of radical transformation does occur, to be sure—Henry Miller's move to Paris illustrates this. Moving to a new place affords us the opportunity to make changes in our lives, but it is we who must make those changes; they don't happen automatically, as the lives I discuss in these pages illustrate. Still, we seem to need to believe that these positive changes will happen effortlessly, regardless of the fact that we must realize, from observing ourselves and others, that no dream house will so radically transform us, that no such domestic Eden exists without our effort to make it so. Our happiness—or lack thereof—is caused by a far more complicated set of circumstances than where we've chosen to live, although this choice can radically alter our lives, for better or for worse.

Remarkably, people rarely believe moving can adversely affect us. (D. H. Lawrence admitted this, but only once, so far as I can tell. Elizabeth Bishop seemed to believe this at the end of her life.) Or that after a honeymoon period, we might revert to the kind of life we've led before, though in a different place, regardless of new opportunities. Still—and sometimes by accident, sometimes by design—many of us, like Henry Miller, do find happiness, a newly meaningful existence, even, perhaps, what feels like the birth of a new self, because of an advantageous move.

In each chapter, I examine one significant aspect of the subject of moving, largely through the testimony of creative personalities: imagining life in that special house; searching for—and finding—it; the hard work of packing and changing residence; living in that transitory period after moving; making a house into a home; forced moves, feeling homeless, choosing to live a wanderer's life; making profound changes in a life by connecting to a new place. In the last chapter, I describe my own moving history— and I suggest that anyone planning a move ponder the significance of their earlier moves and what they truly need in a home so they can make wise choices and, after, ease the transition to a new place.

An unexpected bonus of researching this book was learning how an interest in domestic arrangements almost always enhanced the well-being and creativity of the people whose works I read. Biographies of famous figures tend to describe their public lives, their accomplishments, and their legacies but relegate their interest in finding a home that suits them, interior decoration, or household renovation to paragraphs or footnotes, giving a false sense of how creative people live. Still, their private papers—their letters, journals, and memoirs—are packed with these stories. I was surprised to learn just how often Virginia Woolf wrote detailed descriptions of dream houses, the logistics of her moves, her beloved special possessions and the hard work of packing them, her shopping excursions for household furnishings. This, from a writer commonly thought to live only for the literary life.

I learned that you can create a new paradigm about how human beings function psychologically while spending much time furnishing an apartment and collecting artifacts (Sigmund Freud). That you can write a series of novels that are major experiments in form while buying and selling houses—"flipping" them, on occasion, to make money (Virginia Woolf, who turned out to be more interested in real estate than any other writer in this book). That you can write a landmark work about how a working-class man becomes a writer while moving into friends' flats in Paris and paying, in trade, by cooking (Henry Miller). That you can establish a new esthetic for your poetry while gazing out the windows of your new suburban home (Eavan Boland). That you can write a novel about an aged woman moving into a dream house while you fix up a wrecked old castle (Vita Sackville-West). That you can write political poetry while searching for a house in a perfect landscape to shelter your family (Percy Bysshe Shelley). That you can craft some of the most finely wrought poems in the English language and still bake all kinds of bread and cakes after moving into a lover's house in Brazil (Elizabeth Bishop). That you can write novels challenging the status quo and still whitewash your walls and sew curtains for a rented cottage (D. H. Lawrence). That you can think deeply about another way of looking at the human psyche while building your own home with your own hands (Carl Jung). That you can write a series of novels in a different voice from one you've used before while learning what objects you need on your tables to stimulate your art (Marguerite Duras). That you can pen poems and memoirs about a lover's dying while tending to the business of refurbishing a very old house (Mark Doty).

Perhaps the most important personal outcome of my writing this book is that my father and I talked about my family's moving history during the last months of his life, and I learned what I never before knew, what I would never had known had I not asked him about what he'd never before revealed. As he told me what he remembered—about my grandparents' coming to the United States, about his many moves as a poor boy through Hudson County in New Jersey as his family kept one step ahead of creditors, his settling in Hoboken, New Jersey, with my mother in an apartment they decorated while World War II raged in Europe, our moving to the "promised land" of Bergen Country after the end of the war—we forged a strong bond we'd never before shared. I am only sorry that I was not interested in these stories long before. I learned that asking an elderly family member to relate their moving history unleashes a stream of remembrances, and that these are important and must be preserved. These stories became the most important gift my father gave me before he died.

The last time we met before he became incapable of speech, my father showed me a book he had found containing a photograph of a Catholic church in the neighborhood in Hoboken where my mother and he lived after he came home from World War II. My mother had moved to this new apartment while he was away, and until he returned, he'd never seen it. The image of one church prompted him to tell me the final and perhaps most significant story about his—and my—moving history.

In the story, he's coming back home to the United States

from an island in the Pacific by boat, train, ferry, and bus. He gets off the bus carrying his sea bag and walks down the street past the church that appears in the photo, down just a few blocks more, and around the corner to the tenement on Fourth and Adams Street in Hoboken where I'm living with my mother. My mother and I have moved there since his deployment; we're no longer living in the apartment the two of them refurbished together before their marriage. This is the first time he'll see what will become his home for the next several years.

"Only it wasn't my home, you see," he tells me. "It was yours and your mother's. I never felt I belonged there, and I couldn't wait to move. So many men like me came back to places they'd never seen before where they didn't feel as if they belonged. But it took three years for us to save enough money to leave that apartment. In the meantime I made the best of it. Or maybe I didn't make the best of it, I can't remember now, but I probably took it out on you. But that place never felt like home."

My father felt like the doppelgänger of the man who had gone away. He pretended to be the man he'd been; tried to splice his life into ours; missed the other place, his "real home"; felt he'd lost the art of living in a civilized place.

When he returned home from the war, he didn't come home, he said. He came back to the *idea* of home, a place where the war could be forgotten, where he could pick up his life where he'd left it off, to a place that could soothe and heal the pain he'd lived through but was not yet willing—never was able until near the end of his life—to discuss.

ONE

"A Balm to Cure All Ills"

Dream Houses

A PERFECT PLACE . . .

You're restless, dissatisfied. You tell yourself that everything wrong with your life is because of where you're living. You think, *If I move, find another place to live, a better space, everything will change.* You believe a new place will change you. You'll spend more time relaxing. Have your friends over for dinner. Practice the piano in the evening instead of collapsing exhausted in front of the TV. You'll read more. Organize your photographs. Meditate. Work out every day. You think that if you move, you'll be nicer to your partner, more attentive to your family.

In the moves I imagine myself making, I'm always living in a perfect place. A house that doesn't leak during heavy rains. One with no musty smells in the basement. One without walls that crack and need repair. A home without a filthy oven that needs cleaning. A place where there will be no health problems, no marital problems, no financial woes, no income tax, no work that feels banal and boring.

Throughout my life, as I've walked down one street or another, either in my hometown or in the places I've traveled, I've looked into the windows of houses and imagined myself living there. I imagine the sun shining through these windows in a way that it doesn't in the house I now inhabit. I think about how, in these new places, I will become the self I have not yet managed to be. Thinking like this helps me stop thinking about the problems I face in my work and in my life. If only I could live in this brick house with the lovely side garden, in this clapboard house with the solarium, in this apartment overlooking Central Park, in this whitewashed cottage overlooking the Adriatic, then I could do what I haven't yet done: write a historical novel, knit a modular coat combining all the colors of the rainbow, bake a perfect artisanal bread, listen to all Beethoven's late quartets, and finally, finally read all the writings of Proust. I never think about the people who currently live there, their joys and sorrows; I never think about what life is like for them or the challenges they face. I never recall I've felt pretty much the same wherever I've lived—the tiny apartment when I was in my twenties or the mock Tudor where I spent thirty-plus years.

I never consider why I don't accomplish all I desire where I live now or realize that if I lived in this imagined perfect place, I wouldn't do any of these things either, for real life (the demands of keeping house, of work, of family life) would encroach on me here just as in every other place I've lived. And where I am right now is where I must face whatever this dream of moving helps me elide.

I've lived in seven places, but in my imagination I've lived in far more. In Sicily, I climb up the steep slope of Monte San Giuliano to Erice, an ancient hilltop village. I stay in a splendid hotel at the summit, a former castle. Through its keyhole windows on a clear day you can see the coast, the salt flats at Trapani. When fog settles over the village, everything below disappears. Now this village is the only place in the world.

As I walk the twisting, narrow medieval streets, the only sound is conversation—cars are banned from the historic village center. How different from my town with the incessant whine of a nearby highway. In my imagination I move here as I've moved to so many places I've visited.

Here I would live in a tiny stone house overlooking the valley and the sea. It would have a courtyard, a large balcony with a riot of bougainvillea, and a wrought iron table and chairs for outdoor dining. I'd walk to the local market, choose among several varieties of artichokes, which I'd fry Roman style. I'd buy fresh almonds, cherry tomatoes, spring garlic, a bunch of basil with tiny leaves to make Trapanese pesto. The supper would come together easily. I'd linger over a glass of Cerasuolo wine.

In this place my life would change. It would not be like Buckaroo Bonzai says in *The Adventures of Buckaroo Bonzai Across the 8th Dimension*, "Wherever you go, there you are." All my daily worries—about my work, my family's health, the degradation of the planet—would vanish. Here I'd never rush; I'd live in the moment. I'd accomplish less but I'd enjoy myself far more. I'd attend medieval festivals, Renaissance music concerts, Easter processions. My daily walks would take me through the village to its massive walls.

But this fantasy is dangerous because it makes me dissatisfied with my life no matter how satisfying it is.

There is no place in this fantasy for what living here would really entail. The loss of privacy, a life lived under constant scrutiny, the conformity of behavior, the gossiping neighbors gathered outside the *fruitteria* commenting on your every move. The difficulty of carrying provisions up steep cobblestones slicked by mist. The lack of a good bookstore, a community of English speakers, a place to work.

THE PERFECT HOUSE . . .

In 1923, Virginia Woolf is living at Hogarth House in Richmond, a suburb of London. She writes a diary entry. She's restive, she doesn't know why. She wants to write differently, read more, have meaningful conversations. All this will be possible, she writes, if she finds "a perfect house"; there she'll "arrive at some conception of the meaning of all things."

Whenever Woolf feels dissatisfied with her work, her psyche, her personal relationships, she imagines herself living in a better place. She knows this. Still, she believes that in this new place everything in her personal life will work itself out, everything perplexing in her writing will resolve itself. Now she wants to live where she can engage in philosophical inquiry, probe the meaning of life beyond appearances. She can't imagine doing this living in suburban Richmond.

Woolf calls her compulsion to move "this ancient carrot before me," a trait she possessed from childhood. She understood its origins, knew it persisted because she'd believed if only she could escape her parents' home in Hyde Park Gate, with its Victorian strictures on her behavior, her life would be freer, happier, more meaningful. Though she adored her parents, she wanted to escape the tyrannical ways of her father, Sir Leslie Stephen. And she had also been sexually abused there by her half brothers Gerald and George Duckworth. She knew the only way to escape their incestuous attentions was to live elsewhere.

Early, she began to call the house in Hyde Park Gate a cage

where she was kept locked inside with dangerous beasts. To Woolf, "home" meant a place where you were controlled and abused, a place you had to flee. So she began to imagine a home without constraint or mistreatment where life could be safe, unfettered, and free.

She imagined an idyllic place "without one yelp or discord" where peace, freedom, joy, and sensuality reigned. A place where she could be powerful, realize her ambitions, put her needs before a man's. A "jocund world" with a tranquil garden where she could hear "the kiss of the air or the chatter of insects." This was the dream house Woolf searched for—and found—during adulthood.

When she married Leonard Woolf in 1912, though theirs was a complicated marriage, all their households met her stringent requirements for the ideal home where she could be free to do creative work. Imagining such a place when she young was the prelude to her lifelong quest to live in a safe space. This first happened after her father died, when her sister Vanessa made a home away from the Duckworth brothers in a flat in London's Bloomsbury. There Virginia recovered from a breakdown and published her first work.

Woolf believed that moving was a positive experience. Through the years she'd learned that a change of scene energized her, helped her change direction in her work. She wasn't afraid to throw over a settled life, move from one comfortable place to another that captured her fancy, undertake the risks moving entailed.

Dreaming of perfect places, looking for new houses, moving into them, and refurbishing them became her lifelong habit. Moving was integral to Woolf's creative life, inextricably linked to innovations in each successive novel. A change of scene for her always lead to a shift in aesthetic vision, a transformation of literary form.

Woolf said she made "a fetish" of houses. Looking for a dream house was "a source of great pleasure." Her husband, Leonard, though he sometimes complained about his wife's peripatetic nature, also believed moving was beneficial. His remedy for depression was to "move house, develop a new hobby, work with your hands, buy a puppy." He'd moved their household from London to Richmond when Woolf was depressed, believing that moving to the suburbs would cure her.

Moving to Richmond helped Woolf recover, in spite of bombardments during World War I. Still, she missed London terribly and continued to dream about moving back. "Richmond is certainly the place to live," she wrote ironically, "partly because then London becomes so full of romance."

While in Richmond the Woolfs bought a printing press and began the Hogarth Press, permitting Woolf the freedom to write with certainty of publication and without editorial intervention. There she wrote her first experimental works: "An Unwritten Novel," "Kew Gardens," "The Mark on the Wall," and the novel *Jacob's Room*, in which she said she'd found the way "to say something in my own voice." There Woolf developed her portrait of Jacob Archer, who dies during World War I, through the impressions of other characters, an unconventional device.

In 1919, Woolf is visiting Lewes, Sussex. On a whim she asks about available houses and learns there is one, the Round House, newly on the market. It's small, old. "I pricked up my ears," she writes. Woolf finds out where it is and goes to see it.

It's at the top of a rise in the town center. And it's a very strange round house. Woolf is excited, for this is no ordinary house; it's just the kind of eccentric house she's always desired. She can already imagine the pathbreaking books she'll write there.

The elderly owner of the house lets her in. She sees "small rooms, & the view, & the ancient walls, & the wide sitting room, & the general oddity & character of the whole place." She feels something akin to sexual arousal: "I went from one grade to another of desire," she writes, "til I felt physically hot & ardent, ready to surmount all obstacles."

She buys Round House on the spot.

But when Virginia brings Leonard to inspect Round House as owners, they realize the house is unsuitable, that Virginia's passion has overcome reason. It's dark; the bedrooms are small; it isn't secluded; there's no space for Leonard's country garden.

They're unsettled by Virginia's mistake but learn there's an isolated property standing on three quarters of an acre for sale in a tiny nearby village called Rodmell facing the Sussex South Downs. Imagining its advantages, the Woolfs conclude, it "suited . . . exactly."

Virginia bicycles over to the property, called Monk's House. Wanting to spare Leonard another disappointment, she tells herself this time she'll be rational, she'll "keep excitement at bay." Once there, though, she succumbs to the beauty of the garden, the orchard, the house's insularity. She imagines pensive walks among flowering trees, rambles among the Telscombe downs in fine weather. The view across water meadows is exquisite; she sees herself gazing at them as she writes books.

Monk's House, she thinks, will be "a refuge in cold & storm." She knows her life will change here, that she will have "spaces of leisure." She decides they'll have to sell Round House and buy Monk's House. Immediately.

When she meets with Leonard to tell him about Monk's House, she describes the garden full of "cabbages and roses." He imagines tending it, building fishponds, caring for the orchard's cherry, plum, pear, and fig trees. He agrees that, yes, this is the ideal country house.

The Woolfs sell Round House for forty pounds more than they paid and buy Monk's House. Virginia thinks if they'd held on to Round House longer, they could've made even more. She regrets the loss of funds but thrills at the prospect of life in her new home.

In their eagerness, the Woolfs overlooked many of Monk's House's flaws. Refurbishing it became as important a work in progress as Woolf's novels, and she approached the changes with the same rigor as her revisions. They remedied the house's defects— inadequate drainage causing floods in the kitchen, an antiquated kitchen, no earth closet—by installing gutters, a drainage system, and a new kitchen. Leonard, the most intellectual of men, built the earth closet himself.

They undertook projects enhancing the house's charm and Woolf often used her earnings from writing to pay for them. They built a garden room fashioned from the toolshed, a bedroom addition with a skylight so Woolf could stargaze, a writing studio in the garden overlooking the water meadows and the downs.

Woolf furnished her studio sparely with a simple desk positioned facing the view and an easy chair where she penned her early drafts. Outdoors, for fine days, were lounge chairs. It was the writing room she'd dreamed of since childhood. "I long for a large room to myself," she'd written in 1904, "where I can shut myself up and see no one, and read myself into peace." At Monk's

House, Woolf found the solitude necessary to unravel the conundrums in her work; it became the setting of *Between the Acts*, the novel she was writing when she died.

Even after Virginia was happily settled in Monk's House, she still searched for other houses. "There's nothing I enjoy more than looking for houses," she wrote, "and imagining that I am going to find the very thing. . . . You know my passion for sensation." When she heard a neighbor might build a house overlooking their garden, encroaching on their privacy, she looked at a farm for sale in the meadows. The neighbor's house was never built, and Monk's House remained the Woolfs' country home until she died.

When Woolf thought about why she always searched for houses to buy, she noted her restlessness was aroused on the anniversaries of her mother's death. Each year she remembered and sometimes relived that horrifying time when she became a motherless girl of thirteen. It was, she wrote, "the greatest disaster that could have happened."

After her mother's death, Virginia's father, Sir Leslie Stephen, became morbidly depressed, distant, and withdrawn. Stella Duckworth, Woolf's half sister and surrogate mother, cared for him, leaving no one to help thirteen-year-old Virginia with her grief. All the joy in her life vanished and whatever protection her mother had provided against her half brothers' incestuous behavior ceased. As an adult, Woolf knew she dreamed of moving to distract her attention from painful memories, as if the perfect house would erase them and undo the grief and abuse she suffered in childhood. When she thought about moving, she stopped dwelling on the past. "It's odd," she wrote, "how entirely this house question absorbs one."

FORGING AHEAD, TURNING BACK THE CLOCK . . .

In 1923, Woolf decides that even though Leonard doesn't want to leave Richmond, she will look for a house in London. Leonard believes Woolf's continuing sanity depends on the relative quiet of suburban life. He believes the excitement of London contributed to Woolf's breakdown before they moved to Richmond. He's afraid her sanity will be compromised if they move back to the melee of city life.

Woolf argues that she's well enough to move to London and that it will be a propitious change for her and for her work. She knows she'll have to prove this to her skeptical husband, especially because he's happier in Richmond than she is; he's more reclusive, less social.

She thinks about the best arguments she can make to persuade Leonard, writes them in her diary so she won't forget them. She'll argue that she's agreed to stay in Richmond to please him for years; she's wanted to move since 1920. She'll tell him that living in the suburbs has dulled them, made them settled and complacent. In London, they were tastemakers, key members of the Bloomsbury Group, making a profound impact on British culture. If they stay in Richmond any longer, they'll be less likely to move and will become even more stodgy. "Life settles round one," she writes. "Merely to think of a change lets in the air. Youth is a matter of forging ahead." Just imagining this move makes her feel "ten years younger." No one visits them in Richmond, and she feels isolated and lonely; if she wants to see her friends, she has to travel, incurring stress, losing precious writing time.

She's forty-one, feeling "middle aged," no longer vital. She's afraid of a dull, conservative, vapid future for them in Richmond. She feels as caged living in Richmond as she had living in Hyde Park Gate: "I'm tied, imprisoned, inhibited here," she writes.

London would erase the effects of aging; London would turn back the clock. She knows she would feel energized, even younger, in London. Living in the suburbs, she's missing out on all that life has to offer. In London, she could attend concerts, the theater, and lectures, and visit museums: "Everything [would be] near at hand."

She misses the pulsing street life of London, socializing with her friends, letting herself "go & hear a tune, or have a look at a picture, or find something out at the British Museum, or go adventuring among human beings." She misses her London walks. She wants to live spontaneously, "slip in & out of things easily."

Woolf now believes this move is imperative. She imagines the kind of London house—the view through its windows, its spaciousness—that will inspire her, transform her art. Richmond is blunting her creativity; if they stay, she fears she'll never again create anything with her original stamp. All she's doing is pretending to write "something very important" or "reading with a view to a book I shall never write."

On the eve of traveling to London to look for a suitable house, she thinks about what the city means to her: "Thou art a jewel of jewels, & jasper of jocundite—music, talk, friendship, city views, books, publishing, something central and inexplicable, all this is now within my reach."

Woolf looked for houses in Chelsea, Maida Vale, and Battersea before finally finding a desirable one at 52 Tavistock Square in Bloomsbury. Leonard and she would live there for over two decades. She'd lived in Bloomsbury with her sister years before, after their father's death. It was the place where she first tasted freedom. And the jubilation she'd felt then leaving Hyde Park Gate, she felt too leaving Richmond.

The move to this house in Bloomsbury did not disappoint

her. On the first night Woolf spent at Tavistock Square, she looked out her bedroom window and saw the moon. She was tired from the move, disoriented because she was seeing the moon from a different vantage point and the sight of it was "terrifying and new," "dreadful and exciting." She remarked that until this very moment the moon was "veiled" to her; it was the first time she had truly seen the moon.

And the city was just as thrilling as she remembered. "London is enchanting," she wrote soon after settling into her new home. "I step out upon a tawny coloured magic carpet, it seems, & get carried into beauty without raising a finger. . . . One of these days I will write about London, & how it takes up the private life & carries it on, without any effort." She felt her creative spirit awakening; she believed she could "write & write & write now: the happiest feeling in the world." And she did write about her beloved city in *Mrs Dalloway*, that great London novel, begun in Richmond but completely revised after moving. It was a work whose culmination in 1924 depended on her living in London, a novel she was dissatisfied with in Richmond because she felt cut off from the work's setting.

The move to London had electrified her, urged on her progress. As Woolf walked through London, she gathered details for her book: a little girl in a pink frock playing in a park, a flower shop, an airplane trailing an advertising banner, a limousine transporting a dignitary. The houses she saw each day, the people on the street, the sounds of traffic—much she experienced during her London life made its way into the revision of her work.

Nearing the book's completion, she wrote that she was "galloping over Mrs Dalloway." It was "the most satisfactory" of her novels. In evaluating it, she said, "I think it a very interesting attempt: I may have found my mine this time. I may get all my gold out."

Set in London after the end of World War I, *Mrs Dalloway* follows its central character through a single London day. She walks through a park, buys flowers, prepares for a party, entertains a man she'd once thought she'd marry, thinks about aging, remembers her adolescence and a sibling's tragic death, thinks about a girl she'd loved. It follows, too, the last day in the life of the war veteran Septimus Smith, who kills himself; he might have been a poet had he not been so scarred by war.

Woolf had turned the dream of living in London into a reality. London provided the stimulation she needed and changed her attitude toward writing. It changed her work; it urged her to the completion of an experimental design, unlike anything she'd written. As she broke free from her conventional life in Richmond, she felt energized and her work benefited immeasurably.

During her first winter at 52 Tavistock Square, London continued to dazzle her. "A London winter," she wrote, "is full of bright rooms, passages through dark streets to scenes of brilliancy."

Dividing her time between Monk's House in Rodmell and Tavistock Square in London, Woolf learned, suited her competing needs for solitude and repose and for excitement and stimulation. Both places became necessary to Woolf's art throughout her life; both became settings for her art.

THIS ISLE AND HOUSE ARE MINE . . .

On a day when I'm visiting Viareggio in Italy, I come upon a monument memorializing the drowning death of Percy Bysshe Shelley at sea. His body washed up on this shore, and it was on these sands that his body was cremated.

I knew that Shelley had drowned in a boating accident while trying to sail home during an unanticipated violent storm. I'd read how a friend snatched Shelley's heart from the pyre and gave it to his wife, Mary Wollstonecraft Shelley, and how she had kept it with her until her own death. But I didn't know he'd been cremated at Viareggio.

A few days later I'm in San Terenzo searching for Shelley's last home. In the distance I see an imposing white colonnaded house very near the road. "How would you like to live in that one?" my husband asks, playing our travel game. We don't yet know it's Casa Magni. "No," I say. "Even from this far away, it gives me the creeps."

We dash across the road to see this monstrosity of a house. On the wall is a plaque stating that from its portico, Shelley debarked for his last and fatal sail on the Gulf of Spezia.

While Shelley was living in exile in Italy, he wrote the *Epipsychidion*, a poem describing a house that appeared to him in a dream, the quintessential poem about a dream house.

> *This isle and house are mine, and I have vowed*
> *Thee to be lady of the solitude.—*
> *And I have fitted up some chambers there*
> *Looking towards the golden Eastern air,*
> *And level with the living winds, which flow*
> *Like waves above the living waves below.*

The house in this dream had everything Shelley desired. It was far from the political upheavals that plagued him in England. It was a solitary place in a remote location where a woman—his wife, Mary? a lover?—could dwell with him; it was set in an area of profound and wild natural beauty; it was located on a body of water where Shelley could launch a sailboat to journey toward the proverbial East.

Shelley believed any house he lived in profoundly affected his spirits, his health, and his work. "Who lives in my house in Marlow now?" he wondered. "I am seriously persuaded that the situation was injurious to my health." He believed in the power of a house's aura, that a house could cure him or contaminate him. He thought that living in the right house would change him without any effort on his part.

Shelley had been forced to leave England with Mary, who was his second wife, their two children, Clara and William, Mary's stepsister Claire Clairmont, and Allegra, Claire's child by Lord Byron, because of his radical politics, but also to escape his creditors. In England, Shelley's health was poor and he was deeply depressed; he blamed his ills on living there, on "the smoke of cities, and the tumult of human kind, and the chilling fogs and rain."

The Shelleys were travelers, journeyers, wanderers, always looking for the perfect place to live, always finding the place where they currently resided flawed, always moving on to the next place that might prove to be paradise. Como. Lucca. Bagni di Lucca. Rome. Naples. Florence. Venice. Livorno. Milan. Ravenna. Ferrara. Bologna. Venice. Pisa. And finally, San Terenzo. Shelley thought Italy was the place he'd been searching for where he could establish "a new *kind* of community." But the Shelleys thought, too, that what they wanted might be found not in Italy at all but in Greece: "If Greece be free," Mary wrote, "Shelley and I have vowed to go, perhaps to settle there, in one of those beautiful islands where earth, ocean and sky form the Paradise."

Shelley believed moving to Italy would change everything. "Health, competence, tranquility," he wrote a friend, "all these Italy permits, and England takes away." His chief pleasure in life was "the contemplation of nature," and Italy's natural beauty would satisfy him as no other place could.

"No sooner had we arrived at Italy, than the loveliness of the earth and serenity of the sky made the greatest difference in my sensations," Shelley wrote. He thought Italy would be the balm that would cure him of all his ills. In his letters from Italy, Shelley described the beauty of the country's lakes, rivers, bays, mountains, plains, forests, glens, and waterfalls. Wherever he went, he delighted in the fact that the landscape was the same "the ancients enjoyed."

Shelley believed that living in Italy would affect his writing positively and that he might finally produce a work "stamped with immortality." And while there he felt an "accession of strength" and wrote many of his most significant works: *The Cenci, Julian and Maddalo, Prometheus Unbound, The Mask of Anarchy, Ode to the West Wind, Epipsychidion, A Triumph of Life.*

Near the end of his life, though, he feared he hadn't achieved the level of greatness he desired. Shelley thought his friend Lord Byron had put Italy to better use in *Don Juan,* written during Byron's own Italian sojourn.

Before long, reality intruded on Shelley's fantasy of Italy's curative powers. In his first summer in Italy, in Bagni di Lucca, Shelley admitted having "busy thoughts and dispiriting cares" he wished he could shake off but couldn't. In Naples he described "depression enough of spirits and not good health," though he still clung to the fantasy that "the warm air" of the city was beneficial.

Sometimes Shelley acknowledged that Italy alone wasn't a cure-all, that you must "find your happiness in yourself" for Italy to be "a most delightful and commodious place." Still he reverted to his belief that Italy was salubrious and ignored the real dangers facing his family. He lived in his dream of Italy and denied the risks of its reality: that he and his family could become just as ill in Italy as in England.

Italy claimed the lives of four children in Shelley's extended family. His son William died in Rome of malaria; his sister-in-law Claire Clairmont's daughter, Allegra, in the convent she was consigned to at Bagnacavallo, of typhus or malaria; his ward Elena, left in the care of foster parents, in Naples; his daughter Clara after suffering convulsions in Venice. In a rare admission Shelley attributed Clara's death to a "disorder peculiar to the climate" of Venice. Nevertheless, he maintained that if only he could find the right place in Italy—Naples, perhaps, because of its warmth?—all would be well.

In 1822, when Shelley heard about Casa Magni on the bay of Lerici in the Gulf of Spezia, he believed he'd found the place that had appeared to him in his dream. There, he thought, he could live the life he'd yearned for. He believed that living there would finally reverse his bad fortune—he was still short of money—and that he would at last find peace and solitude. He was detained at Lerici awaiting their furniture being shipped from Pisa, and commanded Mary to take it before someone else did. "Occupy yourself instantly in finishing the affair," he wrote.

Casa Magni was a white stucco house with a wide loggia and seven open arches standing close to the sea. The Shelley clan moved into the house in April 1822. Richard Holmes, Shelley's biographer, describes it as the least hospitable house one could imagine, especially ill-suited to the Shelley household. It was far too small for the Shelley clan and their friends the Williamses, who joined them in May, having arrived in Lerici without accommodation, desperate for a place to stay. It contained only three habitable rooms for the five adults and three children who now inhabited the place. Food, household supplies, and mail had to be ferried from a distance. Mary was expecting and there was no doctor nearby. And it was dangerously close to the sea. The "howling wind" seemed to be ever present, and the sea "roared unremittingly." A visitor remarked it was nearly impossible to sleep on nights when there were rough seas—the sound of the swells breaking on the beach sounded "like the discharge of heavy artillery."

Moving to Casa Magni, even for the spring and summer, as they intended, made no sense. But Shelley's desire to inhabit his presumed dream house distorted his capacity to assess what his family needed. The house was in that wild and out-of-the-way place inhabited by a handful of fisher folk Shelley yearned for. And there was the "divine bay" just beyond the house where Shelley could sail.

After their move to Casa Magni, Shelley dwelled on the scenic beauty surrounding his new home, its landscape of promontories, cliffs, and coastal volcanic rock with a view of a ruined castle set in a forest of pine and ilex. Though he witnessed severe storms—gale-force winds and violent squalls—Shelley insisted the place was invariably "soft and sublime." No doubt he underestimated the danger of sailing its waters, especially given he'd never learned to swim.

But he wasn't writing. Shelley attributed this to the force of Lord Byron's presence in Italy, diminishing his belief in his own creative capacity. Instead of penning a powerful piece of work, Shelley wrote begging letters to procure money from friends to supplement the family's meager income. He read Spanish dramas, listened to musical performances, built a small boat with his friend Edward Williams, sailed, fished.

Shelley was so in love with the place he hoped summer would never end and that autumn, when their lease expired, would never come. He remarked that if Mary liked Casa Magni as much as he did, he could be induced "never to shift my quarters."

But Mary despised the place from the first, although she did not insist they leave. She was pregnant, ill, and unhappy. She called it "a dungeon"; she felt imprisoned. She feared what might happen there; she warned a friend to stay away.

Quite possibly her foreboding was exacerbated by Shelley's flirting with Williams's wife. Shelley enjoyed their joint household; he believed they were living "so intimately, so happily." But Mary had always wanted a more conventional life with Shelley, apart from hangers-on. At Casa Magni she chafed at Shelley's insistence on having an extended household of like-minded friends and women Shelley could dazzle. After Shelley's death, Mary would write, "No words can tell you how I hated our house and the country around it."

Shelley's dream of Casa Magni soon turned to nightmare. Mary suffered a near-fatal miscarriage, and because no doctor was available, Shelley cared for her himself. He made her sit in an ice bath to stanch the bleeding; this saved her life. But she was weak and convalescent for months. She believed she had lost her child because of their reckless move to Casa Magni. She regretted succumbing to Shelley's insistence that they move because he had found his dream house.

After Mary's miscarriage, Shelley began having hallucinations. Just before Shelley's fatal voyage, his friend Williams witnessed one: "He grasped me violently by the arm, and stared steadfastly on the white surf that broke upon the beach under our feet. . . . 'There it is again—there!' He recovered after some time, and declared that he saw, as plainly as he saw me, a naked child rise from the sea, and clap its hands as in joy smiling at him." Williams believed these were prompted by Shelley's feelings of responsibility for all the children's deaths.

Shelley came to believe that Casa Magni was haunted and that the house itself was trying to harm him. He "sees spirits and alarms the whole house," wrote Williams. During one delirium Shelley imagined the bodies of the house's inhabitants "stained with blood"; he imagined the sea rising, "flooding the house and it is all coming down."

Then the sea that Shelley believed would always be benign finally claimed him. His boat foundered in heavy seas; it filled with water and sank. Shelley didn't have a chance. Ten days later his body washed up on the beach at Viareggio.

In one of his last letters from Casa Magni, Shelley wrote, "My boat is swift and beautiful. . . . We drive along this delightful bay in the evening wind, under the summer moon, until the earth appears another world. . . . If the past and the future could be obliterated, the present would content me so well that I could say with Faust to the passing moment, 'Remain thou, thou art so beautiful.'"

Shelley's search for the perfect house prevented him from caring for himself and his family and furthering his work. For what could possibly go wrong in the perfect house that he had imagined, sought, then found?

AGAIN, THE FANTASY . . .

It is early spring, two and a half years since I've moved to Montclair, New Jersey. I feel settled, at peace. It has taken me this long to feel at home.

So far the spring has been extraordinary—a string of warm, sunny days and cool evenings. I've taken time from my writing on a beautiful Friday afternoon to take a walk with Pam Satran, a new friend. Today, as we walk, we talk about moving. I tell Pam about the sometimes overwhelming sense of loss I felt when I first moved—of old routines, familiar spaces, dear friends, the self I left behind. Pam reminds me moving can also be about hope, change, possibility. I tell her this is the last move I'll make. "Don't be so sure," she chides. "You can't predict the future. You can't know how you'll feel in a few years."

Pam is right. Her novel *Suburbanistas* is about the mutability of the self, about how a move can provoke positive change, as it did for Virginia Woolf. In Pam's novel, a famous actress comes back to her hometown—one much like Montclair—from Los Angeles after her mother's death to sell the house she has inherited and to settle her mother's estate. While staying in her mother's house, her childhood home, she begins to rediscover the more authentic self she'd left behind to pursue her dreams of fame and fortune. She decides to leave L.A. and move back to her hometown.

At first she buys a mansion high on a hill, the kind she'd yearned for as a girl, the kind that inspired her dream of success. But she decides if she moves into it, she'll become the person she'd been in Hollywood. She decides instead to live in her childhood home. Here she becomes a better mother, more attuned to her daughter's needs, and a woman capable of a deep friendship. Something about living in the old familiar place fractures the layers of artifice she's built around her true self.

Pam and I are walking on one of my favorite streets in Montclair. On the corner is a house I always notice on my walks in this part of town. Today there's a For Sale sign in front.

"Oh my God," I say. "I love this house." What I don't say, because I am afraid Pam will laugh, is that I'm dreaming of buying this house. She reads my thoughts. "Didn't you say you'd never move again?"

The house is a Victorian painted in shades of warm light greens, creams, and reds. It sits well on its corner lot, and there's enough room behind it for a garden. I imagine myself sitting on its wide front porch in a wicker rocking chair in the summer, sipping lemonade with mint, reading a novel by Amitav Ghosh. This is the same fantasy I had when I first saw the front porch of the house where I live now. And I do sit there often reading. But not nearly as much or as languorously as I'd imagined. I've changed houses, yes, moved into my dream house, but my recalcitrant self hasn't changed that much. Would it if I moved again?

I see a chimney, so there could be fires in a fireplace near which I could sit in an armchair and read Proust during cold winter evenings, though I've yet to light a fire in the fireplace in our new house. But what I love most is the room way up top with a circle of windows looking out into old trees. This would be my study. I imagine it to be a small room with a window seat I'd fill with colorful, plump, comfortable pillows. I'd recline there and read. I'd place my desk facing those windows, and I know words would come effortlessly, more so than they do now.

I want this house, want it more than where I'm living—though I'd wanted that house as much as this when first I saw it. Though the house I'm living in now was—is—my dream house, and I shouldn't want to move, I begin to chart its defects. As I do this, I'm ashamed. I know it's madness, know I'm diminishing my pleasure by unfavorably comparing my house with this one. And I know that I'm doing it because it's less than a year since my father died and thinking about moving again will—I imagine—dampen the pain of mourning his death, which has not diminished with time.

I see my father sitting at the table in the kitchen of the house where I now live during his last visit, sick, weak, unable to rise from the table without assistance, and I wonder if moving elsewhere will erase these painful memories. And I remember him, a young man, striding into our apartment in Hoboken after a long day's work, remember the three-room unheated cold-water flat with a shared toilet without a bathtub or shower where we lived, and tell myself to be grateful for what I have, and who do I think I am to want even more than I have now, and that I am engaging in what I find reprehensible: pursuing a desire that I imagine can quell my sorrow. But it won't; I know it won't.

And as if Pam has read my thoughts, she says, "You know, of course moving isn't always positive. Moving, especially if you move a great deal, can be something else too. Sometimes people move instead of looking at the problems they're having where they are. Sometimes people think that if they change where they're living, that everything else will change. And usually it doesn't. Sometimes I think that you have to stay in a place for a very long time to get to know who you are and to face what you don't like about yourself. Sometimes I think that moving is a phony substitute for making real change."

Still, after our walk ends, when I get home, I call a Realtor. She says she'll stop by with information about the Victorian. As I hang up the phone, I know I won't go see it, I won't buy it, I'll stay where I am. For me, pursuing this dream would be detrimental.

But in those moments when I passed the house with Pam, I'd already moved. I'd started living there. And I was living there differently from the way I live in my own home. I was spending more time doing what I love—cooking, knitting, reading. I was slowing down, lingering for hours on one or another of the house's porches. I was letting the house change me. The woman who lived in that house would cook complicated things—boeuf en daube, pot au feu, salmon en croûte—I'd never made in my own kitchen.

And I see that, yes, Pam is right. Although moving can be about loss, it can also be about change, hope, possibility—even if the move is only imaginary. And I see too that dreaming about moving is always about desire: wanting something other than what you have; being someone other than who you are; living someplace other than where you live; experiencing life in a new way.

But there is a flip side to this, as Pam warned. For if we believe that moving to another place will fulfill our desires, we admit too that where we live now and who we are in this moment are not completely satisfying. Is this urge to move linked to our incapacity to want what we have rather than have what we want? Is this restlessness linked to what the philosopher Alain de Botton calls "status anxiety," measuring your self-worth by your possessions rather than by your character? "Every time we yearn for something we cannot afford," he writes, "we grow poorer, whatever our resources. And every time we feel satisfied with what we have, we can be counted as rich, however little we may actually possess." The simplest way to satisfaction, says de Botton, is to curb our desires.

TWO

"A New and Better Way of Life"

House Hunting

THE DREAM OF OWNERSHIP . . .

There is a television show about moving I'm sure you've seen or heard of, for it's extremely popular. It's called *House Hunters*, and it must be popular because it fulfills some deep-seated need— to live vicariously through other people's moves—because on the surface there isn't much there. During each episode, an ordinary person or couple show viewers where they currently live and relate what they like or dislike about their home—the friendly neighborhood, the backyard where their kids can play, the cabinets in the kitchen; the small bathroom, the cramped kitchen without enough counter space, the dark and gloomy living room, the lack of closet space.

Then they describe what they'd like in a new home. Typically, two sinks in the master bath, a kitchen big enough for the whole family to cook in, a walk-in closet, a backyard big enough for a pool, hardwood floors throughout. They talk about how their lives will change when they find their dream house: they'll spend more time cooking together; they'll sit outside and relax; they'll have their friends over for barbecues; they'll play with their kids in the family room. They anticipate embarking on a new and better way of life, spending more time doing what they haven't done before, as if their current place itself has prevented them from doing what they love. In this show people move for positive reasons only. It's a sanitized version of the American dream.

Enter the real estate agent who after talking to these people for a short time seems to know just what they want and just where to find it. We see them being taken through one, two, three houses or apartments. Some are within their budget; some are under; a few are "a reach." Some places are in move-in condition, some need a little work, a few are run-down and need a lot of work.

The would-be buyers enter the front door, they walk through living rooms, stand in kitchens, peek into closets, appearing to spend less time on the most significant purchase they'll make in their lives than they might spend picking out a wardrobe item. The agent says, "You have to see the kitchen"; "Let's look at the master suite"; "There's a nice yard out back that you will love." The would-be buyers say, "That's nice"; "We can work with this"; "We wanted something a bit bigger."

After a commercial, the buyers reveal which house they've chosen and why. The couples are always shown to be in accord, or one has come round to the other's way of thinking. We never see any hemming and hawing, hysteria, frenzy, or pitched battles. There's nothing like what Virginia Woolf described after she and her husband looked at houses in Mecklenburgh Square in London: "O dear!" she wrote. "We quarrelled almost all morning. . . . I explode: & L. smoulders."

The buyers put in a bid, sign the papers, smile. They're nervous but controlled. They await word to see if their bid's been accepted. The phone rings; they answer. "We got it!" Hugs and kisses all round.

Flash-forward to a short time later: They buyers are settled in their new home. They're in their new living room with their old furniture (it looks much better here) or with the new furniture they've bought for the new space (it's come on time and is the right color and wasn't damaged). Their pictures are on the walls; their books on the shelves; their clothes in closets (no boxes are waiting to be unpacked). They talk about how great their new home is, how much they love their neighborhood, how they've already made friends and had barbecues. (There are no dogs barking across the street, no boiler explosions, no crazy neighbors.) They talk about how it took hard work but how they wouldn't trade their new home for the world.

In TV land, in the unreal world of reality TV, the house-hunting experience is calm, not chaotic; clear-cut, not confusing and disorienting; neat, not messy; easy, not exhausting. The people shown know what they want, they go out to find it, and they get it. In the family's new dream house, the past is left behind, the future filled with possibility. The American dream of home ownership (more and more difficult to realize with each passing year), of upward mobility, of the idea that the purchase of durable goods always converts into newfound happiness is reenacted day after day.

And who wouldn't want to believe it? Who wouldn't want to think that our mobility as a culture, our moving from one place to another, our search for a home is as uncomplicated, unambiguous, predictable, and serene as this show depicts it to be? Who wouldn't want to believe in the myth that finding the perfect house is possible and that moving into it, once it's found, invariably brings joy?

ACCENTUATING THE POSITIVE . . .

In his book *Stumbling on Happiness*, Daniel Gilbert explains why people who have chosen a house after a housing search invariably believe they've made the right choice. He describes how human beings act when they engage in experiences that are "inherently ambiguous," like house hunting. Searching for the right house is always both exciting and nerve-racking, and deciding to buy one house instead of another is always a compromise because every house we buy is always both right and wrong for us. "As soon as our *potential* experience," Gilbert writes, "becomes our *actual* experience—as soon as we have a stake in its goodness—our brains get busy looking for ways to think about the experience that will allow us to appreciate it," which is what most people (except for the die-hard pessimists among us) "do well and often." Gilbert has learned that people evaluate whatever they buy more positively after it's been purchased. "People are quite adept," Gilbert says, "at finding a positive way to view things once those things become their own."

But Gilbert's work also suggests it's very difficult for people to predict how they'll feel after they get what they want. Unlike the consistently happy outcomes shown on *House Hunters*, it's very hard to predict how we'll feel when we actually move into the house of our dreams. This is because the only way we have of predicting whether the house we're looking at will be a good home for us is to imagine what living in that house will be like. "Our brains," Gilbert observes, "have a unique structure that allows us to mentally transport ourselves into future circumstances and then ask ourselves how it feels to be there."

When we look at a house, if the house makes a good first impression, we imagine the best of all possible worlds as we walk through it. We imagine sitting in that living room with guests, cooking a hearty soup in that kitchen, taking a long hot bath in that bathtub, snuggling up in that bedroom with a wonderful book. The scenario we script is invariably positive if we've decided on the basis of gut instinct that we want the house.

Still, as Gilbert warns, "Our ability to simulate . . . future circumstances is by no means perfect. . . . We fill in details that won't really come to pass and leave out details that will." We imagine gatherings we'll never host, meals we'll never cook, moments of relaxation we'll never have. We leave out how we'll struggle up those steep basement stairs with a huge load of laundry, how we'll have trouble sleeping because our bedroom faces a busy street, how we'll want to escape the dark kitchen as soon as possible after Sunday breakfast. It seems miraculous, given our incapacity to predict what will please us, that we ever find a place that suits us or are satisfied living in the places we choose.

WHO WE REALLY ARE . . .

Vita Sackville-West's 1931 novel *All Passion Spent* is about Lady Slane's quest for a new home after her husband's death and illuminates the business of finding a home in an unexpected and informative way. Lady Slane had always been the perfect wife, performing all the duties expected of a partner of a public figure, the Earl of Slane, career diplomat, former cabinet member, former prime minister, and viceroy to India. But through the years she'd considered how she might live more authentically if she survived her husband and what she wanted and needed in a home of her own, freed from the need to maintain appearances as she had to while he was alive.

As a new widow, Lady Slane moves quickly and decisively to find her dream house. In her search, she reveals the private self she's kept hidden for decades, which isn't like the public persona she'd adopted nor like the submissive, dull-witted, incapable woman her children believe her to be. The novel provides a splendid guide to how we can understand what we really need in a home, and how we can ensure it delights us and satisfies our deepest needs. Rather than *imagining* what will please her and searching for a home on that basis, Lady Slane instead considers what *truly* satisfies her. The philosopher Alain de Botton writes that we risk forgetting what we need in a home, and believing we need what won't make us happy. Lady Slane knows she will choose a home to reflect her genuine self because she's taken the time to learn who she really is. She knows too that no house will magically change her; she will have to live differently in whatever house suits her if she wishes to be happy.

Just two days after her husband's funeral, Lady Slane sets out to find a house where she can live her own life, not the "life of others." She has refused her children's attempt to arrange her life by offering to house her each in turn, for she doesn't want to continue pleasing them rather than herself. Nor does she want to live in the center of London, where she'd be forced to continue the public life she associates with strife and competition, not peace and serenity. She wants solitude and privacy to live her life as she chooses, not as dictated by her children or convention.

Against her children's wishes, she sets off alone on the London Underground to Hampstead Heath on the fringes of the countryside. She knows her children are angry at this show of independence, but she is at an age—she's eighty years old—when, she ruefully admits, there is "so little time left" that postponing one's desires is dangerous. Her plan is to search for a little house she'd seen in Hampstead thirty years before and dreamed of through the years. She hopes it will be available.

"It was a convenient little house," Lady Slane has told her children, "not too small and not too large . . . and there was a nice garden." She'd wanted to rent it then, but it wouldn't have been grand enough for the image her husband wanted to project as a public figure. Now, she believes, it reflects the qualities she's lost touch with and yearns to cultivate—independence, quietude, simplicity.

This excursion in search of a house is Lady Slane's first taste of freedom, anonymity, and solitude in sixty years. She is heady with joy, basking in "the extraordinary sensation of being independent."

Alone on the Underground, she contemplates aging. She resolves to make the most of the time remaining; this entails accepting she will soon die. She realizes she's postponed her dreams because she's denied her mortality; she realizes most people do so because they won't face that difficult reality. She believes this house will accommodate her new way of life: she'll be unconcerned with worldly goods or achievement and simply let herself "be."

Arriving at Hampstead Heath, she thinks of nothing but "finding the house, *her* house." And she does, and it's as she's remembered, and it's empty. Lady Slane wants to rent it and asks the owner, Mr. Bucktrout, whether he believes the house will suit her. He replies, "Ah, but the question is, will you suit *it?*" This forces her to think about her search for a home in a new way: she recognizes she'll have to change if she wants to live her desired life in this house; simply moving will not be sufficient.

The caretaker lets her in. She waits for him to leave so she can be alone to experience the house. She doesn't want to be distracted by conversation. Lady Slane stands quietly, feeling the curious sensation "common to all who remain alone for the first time in an empty house which may become their home." In these moments, the house reveals itself and she ponders whether the marriage of inhabitant and house will be fortuitous.

Lady Slane realizes a house is "an entity with a life of its own," imbued with as much spirit as a human being. Too often, she thinks, people force their will on a house. Instead, she wants to discover the kind of life this house will require of her. She will have to learn how to live from it, imbibing its spirit.

She hasn't wanted to see the whole house, only the bedroom and garden, where she believes she will spend most of her time. The bedroom faces south and is washed with sun. Below she can see a small grove of peach trees. Standing in the deserted bedroom, Lady Slane realizes this might be the room she'll die in. She realizes that house hunting is inevitably a memento mori, a reminder of our mortality and of time's passage. Still, she knows she is coming here not to die but to live more fully.

Some ivy has grown through a chink in the window frame, some bits of straw have blown onto the floor, a colony of spiders has taken up residence. These don't upset her; they fill her with serenity, for they represent what she now wants, "to merge with the things that drifted into an empty house." She too would "drift down the passage of years, until death pushed her gently out and shut the door behind her." She knows she'll sit in the garden to witness nature, to watch the progression of the seasons. At this stage of her life she wants to understand her relationship to the rhythms of the natural world and how small a role human beings play in nature's larger scheme.

Lady Slane has found her home. Here she will try to live truly rather than merely exist. Here she will try to suit this house and learn "nonstriving." And she does.

Lady Slane disposes of her wealth, giving her artistic treasures to the public and her money to the poor. She believes her possessions have prevented her from living a creative life, and she now wants to understand what that kind of life might entail.

She becomes friends with Mr. Gosheron, the fix-it man who teaches her that houses have souls and that rushing about is useless. She becomes more intimate with her maid, Genoux, who teaches her about how to live meaningfully despite loneliness. She develops a deep affection for the house's owner, Mr. Bucktrout, who understands her need for quiet. These friends aren't members of her social class, yet they become more important to her than her own children.

When he visits, Mr. Bucktrout brings bouquets of flowers he's grown and arranged. They're a lovely gift because they represent his labor and concern for her. Like her, he loves the play of light on flowers in a vase in a sun-filled room. During their visits they talk about how it's "better to please one person a great deal than to please a number of persons a little, no matter how much offence you give"; how one must seize the moment because "life is so transitory"; how it's "no good in thinking of yesterday or to-morrow." In this house Lady Slane is the happiest she's ever been; here with these people she doesn't feel woefully inadequate but rather intelligent, capable, and confident.

THE DEEPEST ROOTS OF ALL . . .

Vita Sackville-West began writing *All Passion Spent* soon after she'd hunted for and found a new home for herself and her family—Sissinghurst, a ruined castle—in the Kentish Weald. Sackville-West's fictional portrait of Lady Slane's joy at finding exactly the right place to spend her last years was drawn from Vita's own experience, from the feelings she had after discovering

Sissinghurst and learning it was for sale. Her exhilaration was so great that she wrote the novel in ten months while attending to all the details of making the wreck of Sissinghurst fit for habitation and of collaborating with her husband, Harold Nicolson, in planning the garden that would become among the most famous in all England.

From soon after she met Harold, a junior member of the Foreign Office posted in Constantinople, Vita began writing him letters about the dream houses they would inhabit when they married. Or, rather, *if* they married. For she and her childhood friend Rosamund Grosvenor were still lovers when Vita and Harold began discussing marriage, although Harold did not know this. Still, Vita knew that *if* she married, it would be to Harold. And she knew that if she married, she'd be faithful to him.

Vita was not altogether sure she wanted to commit to a union she feared would be a sham and force her into a conventional life she believed would be stifling. But Harold was certain that he wanted to marry her and that their marriage would be magnificent—he referred to its prospect as "our amazing marriage"—even though he had no intention of abandoning his homosexual life, about which Vita knew nothing. He saw no conflict between his commitment to Vita and any children they might choose to have and living a private sexual life.

Vita wrote Harold in Constantinople about how they would travel widely after they married but would also have a settled life in a home of their own. Though she would wear "gorgeous clothes and jewels" and act the part of the conventional matron when they visited cities like Rome, when they lived in their own private "little ramshackle place . . . near the sea," her unconventional side would appear and she would be "humble and dirty" and wear comfortable green corduroy. They would swim "before breakfast on a deserted beach in the sun" and take their first meal "in the loggia"; in the evening they would sit and read or do absolutely nothing at all. They would make a garden with "masses and masses of flowers" because their home would be in a climate "where everything grows." Even in these early fantasies of their shared home, solitude was essential to Vita's vision of the ideal place to live; she later celebrated its virtues in a poem called *Solitude*.

Once when Vita was on holiday in Seville, enjoying herself immensely—in Spain she felt an affinity with her Gypsy grandmother Pepita—she wrote Harold that when they married, they would have to live in Seville because it was important for her to live in a place associated with her family's history. "This is the life for me," she wrote. She wanted them to have a simple place in Seville, with just a few rooms; living lavishly was less important than living in a place connected to her ancestors. Gypsies would come and dance for them; they would entertain "disreputable artists"; they would go out dancing and to bullfights, and Vita would outfit herself like Pepita in a "black mantilla and a high comb and carnations."

When Vita and Harold married in 1913, three years after they met, neither acknowledged that their mutual desire for same-sex love might become a problem for them. They set up their first home at Cospoli in Constantinople, overlooking the Golden Horn. There Vita created her first garden. Vita at first accompanied Harold, trying to be the good and faithful wife who buries her own desires—like Lady Slane, who had accompanied her husband wherever his career took him, subverting her desires to meet his needs. Vita drew upon her early married life for creating Lady Slane's experiences. Unlike Lady Slane, though, Vita did not live like this for long.

When Vita and Harold returned to England from Constantinople, they created two homes: one at 182 Ebury Street in London; the other, at Long Barn, a fourteenth-century cottage in the Kentish countryside. Harold loved his "two happy homes." They symbolized his love for Vita and their sons, Ben and Nigel, and what he believed to be the rock-like stability of their marriage. Each was different, suiting different needs: Ebury Street was "rather stern and prim and quiet"; Long Barn "all untidy and tinkly."

In time Vita refused to move with Harold to his foreign postings, unlike other diplomats' wives, and continued to reside in England with their children. She would join him abroad for a few months but was always exasperated by the business and ceremony of diplomacy, writing about her trips and Harold's life ironically in works such as *Passenger to Teheran*.

In 1917 she learned about Harold's homosexual life and infidelities because he had contracted a venereal infection and had to tell Vita so she could undergo treatment. Vita was shattered by Harold's betrayal and deception. She was furious that she alone had abandoned same-sex love and decided that henceforth she would not subvert her desire. So she left Harold, their children, and her homes for an itinerant life with her lover Violet Trefusis.

Even in childhood Vita had seen herself as "liberated, iconoclastic, rebellious, . . . a wanderer." Now she and Violet fled to France, with their husbands initially in pursuit. This event in Vita and Harold's marriage is chronicled in their son Nigel Nicolson's *Portrait of a Marriage*.

In time, though, Vita's love for Harold and their children and her desire for creating a home where she could live a free and unfettered life triumphed. Violet's erratic behavior had made their affair a burden. She returned to Harold and the children, deciding that she would never again permit a grand passion to threaten her home life, her marriage, and the serenity she required to do her work.

But she rewrote the rules of their marriage. Henceforth, traditional domestic life and the sexual side of their marriage would be abandoned. She and Harold would be free to establish relationships outside their marriage. Each would lead separate lives, she as a writer and gardener, at Long Barn, which they'd purchased in 1915, and later at Sissinghurst Castle; and he as a diplomat in France, Persia, and Germany, and later as a member of Parliament in London and a writer at Sissinghurst.

Their home and their marriage, however, would remain the core of their life. Central to their marriage was their desire for each other's support and companionship, nourished by letters, visits, and joint holidays. And they would now need to be honest about their extramarital affairs—one of Vita's would be with Virginia Woolf.

In 1930, Vita and Harold discovered that the land adjoining Long Barn was being acquired by poulterers, which threatened the serenity of their home. So they decided to search for a new place, preferably in the Kentish Weald, which they both loved and where Vita's family had long roots. The Sackvilles had lived there since 1566, when Elizabeth I deeded Knole, one of the greatest houses in England, to her ancestor Thomas Sackville.

Vita had grown up in Knole, a house that is reputed to contain 365 rooms. In both *Knole and the Sackvilles* and *The Edwardians*, Vita wrote that it resembled a "medieval village with its square turrets and its grey walls, its hundred chimneys sending blue threads up into the air," with a kitchen "as wide and high as a cathedral."

As a child, Vita had taken visitors to see the house's show rooms, one containing furnishings made of sterling silver. She had played—often alone—in miles of galleries lined with portraits of her famous forebears, had gamboled over floors "made of the halves of oaks," had sat in chairs "that Shakespeare might have sat on," had fallen asleep in beds where kings and their consorts had lain, had contemplated the lives of the women depicted in scenes on tapestries, had been allowed to play with the "diamond and ruby dingle-dangle" that appeared in a Gainsborough portrait of one of her relatives. As a child and young woman, Vita had written poetry and novels about Knole, her ancestors, and her own place in its long history. As a young woman, Vita had studied the letters, diaries, and other documents in Knole's Muniment Room (these would form the basis for her histories of Knole). In 1912, Vita had described to Harold how her mother let her stay at Knole in her tower room, shutting the world out and locking herself away, giving orders that she was not to be disturbed until the next morning, dreaming "back five hundred years, to the days when the paintings on my walls were new."

Vita and Harold had married in the chapel at Knole. More than six hundred wedding presents—among them, jewels fashioned from emeralds and diamonds, a bust by Rodin—were displayed in the house's Great Hall. Living at Knole had affected Vita profoundly. She had grown into a woman who was, as Leonard Woolf described, "handsome, dashing, aristocratic, lordly, almost arrogant."

Vita tried to explain to Harold her profound and deep love for Knole, which equaled or surpassed her love for her family. She compared it to her love for a beautiful woman who had never completely belonged to her but who nonetheless loved her with "a sort of half-maternal tenderness and understanding." Harold understood his wife's deep attachment to Knole. There was "some sort of umbilical cord" tying her to her ancestral home.

Vita's love for places—Knole, Sissinghurst—was something Virginia Woolf couldn't understand. She once chided Vita that she loved places more than people. Yet Woolf did understand the profound significance of Knole to Vita; *Orlando,* Woolf's love letter to Vita, is set at Knole.

Vita loved Knole passionately. But after her father's death in 1928, Vita, an only child, was prevented by Kentish law from inheriting Knole because she was a woman. For three days only, while her father's body lay in state, until the moment of his burial, Knole belonged to Vita. But afterward the property passed into the hands of her uncle Charlie (Charles Sackville-West), who was married to an American. Vita believed Charlie could never appreciate Knole and railed against the injustice of Kentish law. She wrote to Harold about her fantasy of murdering her uncle. "I want Knole," she wrote. "I've got an idea about it: shall we take it some day? I've taken Dada's revolver. And the bullets." But following her uncle's death, Knole would be inherited by her uncle's son, her cousin, Eddy.

Two years after the loss of Knole, Vita happened upon Sissinghurst, "a complex of ruins, in seven acres of muddy wilderness" in Kent. As soon as she saw it on a spring day in 1930, she "fell flat in love with it." She said that it "caught instantly at my heart and my imagination. I saw what might be made of it. It was Sleeping Beauty's castle."

Vita recognized that the property afforded the kind of privacy she and Harold needed and that they could live there "unmolested." There was ample space for a garden and views across the weald. There was a structure with two towers still standing, reminding her of the tower room at Knole. There was enough space for both of them to have separate bedrooms and sitting rooms and sufficient space for their children and hired help. She told Harold she had found "the ideal house . . . a sixteenth century castle," even though the property was derelict. For years it had been used for billeting prisoners and then as a stable and outhouse for an adjoining farm. There was no heat, electricity, or water. Nor was there one habitable room in what had once been a glorious Tudor mansion.

Harold found an old print of the building and researched its history. He discovered that Vita's family was connected to the place. In the sixteenth century, Sissinghurst Castle had belonged to Sir John Baker, whose daughter Cicely had married Thomas Sackville, whose portrait hung at Knole.

After thinking the matter through, Harold wrote Vita: "(a) . . . it is most unwise of us to get Sissinghurst" because of the cost of rehabilitating it; "(b) . . . it is most wise of us to buy Sissinghurst [because] . . . [i]t is for you an ancestral mansion"; "(c) . . . It is in a part of Kent we like. . . . I could make a lake"; "(d) We like it."

Vita made an offer, of £12,000, which was accepted. It would cost another £15,000 for renovations. As a symbolic gesture toward the garden she envisaged, Vita planted a lavender bush. And she began writing *All Passion Spent*, in which her protagonist's great joy in finding the perfect house—based on one Vita had seen on an excursion to visit Keats's house in Hampstead Heath with Virginia Woolf—replicated Vita's own in finding Sissinghurst. At Sissinghurst, Vita would become increasingly solitary.

Vita and Harold knew that it would take years to turn Sissinghurst into a proper home and to establish a garden, but they also knew they could make it into precisely the kind of home that would suit them. They moved into Sissinghurst in 1932, two years after its purchase; but they were still renovating in 1935, the year when they converted a gatehouse to a library.

They turned what had been the Priest's House into living quarters for their sons and helpers. They redid the South Cottage to house Vita's and Harold's separate bedrooms and bathrooms and Harold's sitting room. They outfitted one tower with a writing room and a newly built fireplace for Vita. Many of their home's furnishings came from Knole—"Persian rugs, glass, silver and ebony mirrors . . . ; Jacobean chests." Although their home was rustic rather than grand, these objects seemed as if they were specially made for Sissinghurst. As a housewarming gift, Woolf gave Vita the handpress that she and Leonard had purchased when they established the Hogarth Press in Richmond; Vita installed it on a landing leading to her study in the tower.

The only place for the family to gather was the dining room, which suited them both. To get from one building to another, they had to walk outside through the garden even in the most severe weather, but that also meant that the garden—which they created together and remains one of the finest in England—was as significant a part of their household as the interior spaces. Harold joked that "when we are old we shall die if we have to go on a long country walk from meal to meal." Vita said she liked that they each had separate quarters and that they had to walk outside.

Years later, in 1948, Harold summed up his feelings about Sissinghurst in a letter to Vita: "Sissinghurst," he wrote, "has a quality of mellowness, of retirement, of unflaunting dignity, which is just what we wanted to achieve and which in some ways we have achieved by chance. I think it is mainly due to the succession of privacies: the forecourt, the first arch, the main court, the tower arch, the lawn, the orchard. All a series of escapes from the world, giving an impression of cumulative escape."

Vita confessed that after marrying Harold and prior to living at Sissinghurst she had felt "rootless," had felt "no permanent attachment" to any of the places where they'd lived. In Sissinghurst, Vita had found a replacement for Knole, and she had found home. Once, while she was traveling in the United States, she wrote her son Ben: "One realizes how much one longs, humanly, for <u>roots</u>, and the deepest roots of all are those one finds in one's own home." After Vita's death, Leonard Woolf remarked, "In the creation of Sissinghurst and its garden she was, I think, one of the happiest people I have ever known, for she loved them and they gave her complete satisfaction in the long years between middle age and death in which for so many people when they look out of the windows there is only darkness and desire fails."

CLAIMING A HOME'S INNER QUALITIES . . .
Alain de Botton in *The Architecture of Happiness* urges us to remember that any home we choose won't automatically make us happy. Vita Sackville-West did suffer bouts of depression at Sissinghurst, the home she believed would bring her the infinite pleasure she describes in her poem "Sissinghurst," but it was her own activity there—writing, gardening—that gave her delight. No matter how special a house's qualities, no house can make us happy or solve but "a fraction of our dissatisfactions." De Botton notes that "tyrants and murderers, sadists and snobs" have often lived in magnificent surroundings.

The houses we search for often represent qualities we lack but aspire to. Thus the person who feels insignificant might search for an imposing house. A perpetually anxious person might search for a home with harmonious proportions. A family that prefers privacy but desires more togetherness might search for a house with open spaces.

But happiness might not come "from what we presume will give us pleasure—large rooms, large closets, beautiful landscaping, expensive fittings." Rather, it might be more humble qualities with "an unostentatious, unheroic character . . . , a run of old floor boards or . . . a wash of morning light over a plaster wall" that will delight us.

To know what to search for we must first learn what we need in a home and also what truly gives us pleasure rather than imagine what we think will give us pleasure. Is it the ability to gaze out the window at a tree in bloom? A window that looks out over the roofs of buildings in a city? A tiny space with a vaulting ceiling where we will feel secure but expansive at the same time? A window seat where we can curl up with a good book? A sunny place to sit at breakfast? Giving up something we might not realize is essential for our well-being (sunlight in a kitchen, say) for something that we think we desire but that does not really suit us (a lavish up-to-date kitchen that faces north, say) might wind up disappointing us rather than pleasing us.

We are, de Botton reminds us, "at constant risk of forgetting what we need" in a home and at constant risk of believing we need things that will not make us happy. The homes we choose can help us commemorate "our genuine selves." But only if we have taken the time to learn what are our heartfelt desires.

Moving into a home embodying the virtues of the self we wish we were may indeed "help us realise our ambition of absorbing [its] virtues," says de Botton. But it can also serve as a sad reminder of how little we have changed despite our move to a new place that we believed would alter our lives. Whatever changes we make will not happen "automatically or effortlessly," regardless of what we imagine. But if we are aware that we're hunting for a house embodying qualities we don't yet possess, then we can begin to work at claiming "the inner quality [the house] embodies." Or to recast what Mr. Bucktrout tells Lady Slane, the question we should ask ourselves is not whether a house will suit us, but rather how we will need to behave to suit it. This requires hard work and introspection.

A SAFE PLACE . . .

Before my father left for the Pacific, he decided he wanted to move my mother and me into a better place. When he thought about moving from the tenement where we lived on Fourteenth Street in Hoboken, he didn't think about moving to a more expensive neighborhood or to a larger or more beautiful apartment. A better place, to my father, simply meant a safer place that was affordable on a sailor's salary. It was wartime; our neighborhood was near the docks and dangerous, filled with carousing enlisted men wanting a good time before they left for battle.

Although my parents lived in what my father believed was the worst part of town, they were house proud and had made the best of a place someone else might have allowed to fall into decrepitude, decorating their apartment as beautifully as if it were in one of the brownstones on the Heights or in one of the elegant apartment buildings on Washington Street. There was rose wall-to-wall carpet in the living room, a sofa and an easy chair with an ottoman upholstered in a deeper shade of rose, a chinoiserie side table that converted into a dining table, a quilted silk comforter for the bed with matching pillow shams, an antique bureau topped with a gilt mirror (passed on to me upon my mother's death), an Italian chifforobe, stylized leaf-patterned wallpaper in shades of beige, soft green, and ivory, and lined drapes for the windows made by my mother on her Singer sewing machine.

My parents decorated this, their first home, before they married, scraping wallpaper off the walls, sanding them, repapering them, my father told me, as they listened to the radio reports describing the German invasion of Minsk. "Shut that damned thing off," my mother would say, not wanting to hear about the progress of the war she suspected would one day take her husband from her. Evening after evening they worked to make this apartment a home, as if by papering walls, laying carpeting, hanging drapes, they could shut out the war, protect themselves, create a space where the violence of the battlefield would not penetrate. To them it was a sacred space: the first place my father slept on a proper bed, not on cots or chairs pushed together in his parents' overcrowded apartments; the first place my mother slept in a bedroom and not on a sofa in the parlor. It was where they nourished their love. It was where they tried to jettison their parents' immigrant pasts and laid claim to their version of the American dream.

My father never found another apartment for us; apartments for let were in short supply during the war. At the end of his life my father told me that he realized he had been searching for the unattainable: absolute safety for his wife and child during wartime.

THREE

"A Home, Dismantled"

Packing Up

LIKE A GHOST . . .

When Stephen King came home from the hospital after being treated for a near-fatal bout with pneumonia, an outgrowth of his near-fatal accident in 1999, when he was hit by a van while he was walking alongside a Maine road, he walked into his office in a converted barn and discovered that, without his knowledge, his wife, Tabitha, had begun to renovate it: "The rugs were gone, and most of [the] books and papers were boxed up." The sight of his office in chaos and his possessions in boxes unnerved him—even though the family wasn't moving. Everything surrounding King during his writing life that helped him feel grounded in space and time, helped him define who he was, had been removed. "I went in there," he said, "and I could barely breathe. I thought, this is what places look like when somebody's died. I thought to myself, this is what it is like to be a ghost."

This unnerving moment, when a familiar, comforting place

becomes something other than what it was and provokes unsettling feelings—so common to people who move—became the seed of his novel *Lisey's Story*. It relates a widow's response to her famous writer husband's death and what she discovers about him as she goes through his possessions. King's feelings about seeing his office in a state of disarray and his possessions in boxes were linked in his mind with his two near-death experiences (the pneumonia and his having been hit by a van while walking); they form the emotional substructure of the novel, which he began while recovering from pneumonia. *Lisey's Story* describes how packing and sorting through possessions prompts us to relive the past and explains why packing to move can be so difficult: it unmoors us and often reveals more than we'd like to know.

AN ITINERANT LIFE . . .

Throughout his life, the sight of suitcases or boxes packed for a move or a change in a familiar room often unleashed uncontrollable bouts of destructive rage in the playwright Eugene O'Neill. Although he never lived in one place for very long and packing and moving were an integral component of his life from infancy, the scene of a home dismantled so unsettled him—no doubt because it recalled all the difficult moves his family made during his childhood, his mother's hatred of these moves, and his parents' vicious battles about them—that he became violent. Once he wrecked his room at Princeton. Another time, upon a return from a trip to Honduras, he went to his parents' suite at the Lucerne, took a machete out of his suitcase, and started "hacking at things all over the apartment, cutting off the legs of tables and chairs." After his marriage to Carlotta Monterey, he "ravaged a room" where she'd installed blue satin wall coverings.

O'Neill's childhood was filled with impermanence. His father, James O'Neill, was an actor, and after his father's enormous success in creating the lead role in *The Count of Monte Cristo*, the O'Neill family lived an itinerant life as the production toured the country. They lived in hotels, his mother, Ella, packing and unpacking their trunks at every stop, trying to care for her family in cramped and unsanitary quarters, despising this way of life. During his first seven years, O'Neill contracted "typhoid fever, rickets (a disease of malnutrition), colic"—all caused by their living conditions.

O'Neill was born in Barrett House, a residential hotel at Forty-third Street and Broadway in New York City where his parents were living; he died in the Shelton Hotel in Boston's Back Bay, where he was living with his wife, Carlotta. Just before his death he cried out, "I knew it! Born in a goddam hotel room and dying in a hotel room."

O'Neill never stayed long in one place. He lived in Honduras; Buenos Aires; England; the Loire Valley in France; California; New London, Connecticut; New York; Cape Cod. His adult life mimicked the itinerant life his mother despised when he was a child. He seemed to be repeating the painful pattern of his past with all this packing and unpacking, not because it enriched his life but because it mired him in the familiarity of pain. According to the biographer Stephen A. Black, "He stayed in no place for very long. To be born and die in hotel rooms suited a life of psychic wandering."

Throughout her life, O'Neill's mother continually complained that because the family moved so much she had "no idea what a home was." She wanted "a fine house on a fashionable street in New York"; instead her husband built Monte Cristo Cottage in New Haven, Connecticut, where the family often spent summers when James O'Neill wasn't touring. It was the closest thing to home O'Neill knew. But to O'Neill's mother, who believed her life had been damaged because the family never had a "proper home," Monte Cristo Cottage didn't count; it wasn't grand enough to suit her. She refused to call it home, refused to have meals prepared, and the family lived there in a state of permanent rootlessness.

O'Neill blamed his father and his birth for his mother's bitterness and her morphine addiction, which often required long stays in a sanatorium or convent. Repeating his mother's pattern, O'Neill became addicted to alcohol—at thirty-seven, he referred to twenty-two years of hard drinking—often drinking as much as a quart of alcohol a day. At the heart of the family's mythology was the idea that an impermanent lifestyle produced these dire consequences.

These issues form the core of O'Neill's *Long Day's Journey into Night*, a play examining the potential consequences of rootlessness for those who crave home. In the play, Mary Tyrone's alienation, profound sense of loss, and addiction are connected to the family's lack of a stable home, to the stress of packing and unpacking, to her transient life. She cannot or will not make friends and so feels "cut off from everybody." She blames her isolation on her husband, James, and his ambivalence, or hostility, to a settled family life, which seems related to his Irish immigrant past. "You don't really want [a home]," she tells him. "You never wanted one." James believes Mary's isolation is caused by her clinging to the memory of life in her father's house. As he tells her, "It is you who are leaving us, Mary."

Near the end of his life, O'Neill bought a cottage on the coast near Boston at the tip of Marblehead Neck "because it reminded him of Monte Cristo Cottage." It had "no real kitchen, no heat, and minimal electric wiring." In buying it, O'Neill was re-creating the abysmal living conditions of his childhood. In an eerie parallel of his parents' quarrels, Carlotta and he argued because she detested the house and he refused to move to a more well-appointed place.

THE RITUAL OF PACKING . . .

Just before our move I'd read *Nomads of the Niger*, about the Wodaabe, a tribe who roam a part of central Niger where water and rainfall is sparse. Who, I thought, would understand the experience of moving better than a nomadic people? The Wodaabe move from one place to another searching for water and better pasture for their livestock; if they didn't move, their livestock would die. Though moving is their way of life, some would prefer a more settled existence. "There's no end to it," one Wodaabe woman remarks. "If only we could rest."

I'd falsely assumed people on the move all the time would be used to it. Yet the Wodaabe's moves are filled with stress and chaos even though the "migration is carefully planned" and there is ritual and order to breaking camp and packing. Calabashes are cleaned, kitchen utensils are gathered, bedding is taken apart, and all is carefully packed on oxen and donkeys, together with bags of millet, sacks of clothing, mats, stools, water bags; the most precious decorative possessions are stashed on top. During packing, there is "the greatest agitation and confusion." In time, though, a "semblance of order" emerges.

The burden of the move falls on the women; loading and unloading the pack oxen and donkeys at the end of each leg of the journey is women's work. The women are also responsible for ensuring that there is food; they "walk for hours in the sun carrying calabashes of milk" on their heads. The stress of the journey causes arguments between the men and women.

But the Wodaabe mollify the intensity of this work with stories of how their life will be much better in the new place: there will be more food; they won't be hungry. Once they establish their new camp, they will have a celebration, showing off their prized possessions in the new location. Anticipating this ritual helps motivate them during the arduous labor of the move.

They also tell stories about other tribal moves, tales that remind them of the connection between their present and past moves, and of the fact that all moves finally end—however briefly. Other stories are told about the moves different peoples have made and about mythic characters, connecting their experience with the world beyond their tribe.

Once the journey is complete, the time comes for ceremony and more storytelling. This is "the blessed period," the settled period, when people can enjoy themselves. The stories that are told once the tribe is settled reinforce their fundamental values and honor their heritage and survival. At this time, the men fashion jewelry and talismans and the women refurbish artifacts they own and arrange them for display.

Remembering past moves, telling stories of past moves, enacting rituals around moves, celebrating the arrival—all these Wodaabe traditions adapted to my own situation, I believed would help me through the difficult transition of my own move.

WHAT HAD BEEN WILL NEVER BE AGAIN . . .

The moment our moving company delivered boxes to our home in Teaneck, New Jersey, where we'd lived for over thirty years, and dumped them on the floor of our living room—the place I retreated in late afternoon to drink a cup of tea and gaze out the stained glass window to the trees beyond our neighbor's house across the street—I began to live in that liminal state that occurs when you move. Before I expected it, that room had transformed into the place I was leaving and stopped being a space I cherished. A flicker of memory: our apartment in Hoboken filled with boxes in preparation for the wrenching move to the suburbs my parents, grandmother, sister, and I made after my grandfather's death.

I thought of all the good times this room had seen—my family gathering here at Christmas for our ritual of taking turns opening presents, writer friends drinking tea and talking shop with me, guests enjoying an after-dinner drink after a home-cooked meal. I felt the passage of time like a wind rushing through the house: what had been here, the life I lived here, would never be again. I thought, too, of all the opportunities for enjoying this room that I'd missed, the fires I hadn't made on rainy fall days, the times I hadn't lingered to watch the sun set through the stained glass window, the journal entries I hadn't made while reclining on the sofa, the knitting I hadn't done in my wicker chair. After the boxes arrived, I entered what the composer and writer Allen Shawn has called the "huge crisis" of moving: "It's actually true," he said, that when you move, "you are losing a part of yourself and you are going to have to rebuild a sense of where your center is." And nothing underscores this more than packing.

On the night of the boxes' arrival, I had a dream, one of those heart-pounding dreams from which you awaken in the middle of the night and that taint the next day and the day after that. In my dream, the boxes come, and there are so many of them they fill up the entire living room, floor to ceiling. They are piled everywhere, on top of the furniture, in the spaces behind. Inside the room there is no light, for the windows are covered by boxes. I see the boxes from the kitchen, try to walk into the living room, realize this is impossible, know I can never remove the boxes, that they'll be there forever. I know I can no longer stay in this house; I must grab my keys, climb into my car, get away. But once I start driving, I have nowhere to go and don't want to go back to the place that had until now been home. In the dream—and this is when I awaken—I drive and drive and drive.

What will I become in my new home? What will become of me?

On the day I begin packing, I realize I'll have to make a decision about everything I own, whether to keep, pack, and move it, or whether to give it to Goodwill or trash it. This realization about the number of decisions I'll be making is so shocking that I stop what I'm doing, sit down, and cry. It isn't the packing that causes me pain: it's that packing forces me to review my entire life—the celebratory times, the painful times. Packing is a full-scale life inspection thrust upon me when my psychic resources are at a nadir. Nothing has prepared me for the agonizing choices I will now have to make.

Stored in our basement and attic, in the nooks and crannies of several closets around the house, are all the objects that have come into my husband's and my possession after the deaths of his parents, my mother, and my sister. Until now we haven't thrown them away; we've coexisted with all this stuff without giving it too much thought. We've moved a box of his mother's personal effects off an extra chair in the basement when we've needed the chair to seat a guest. We've kicked aside his father's toolbox when we've needed to open an old filing cabinet. We've pushed aside my mother's old clothes in the closet to get at our winter coats. We've lifted my sister's photograph albums off the stack of reams of paper when we've needed to refill the printer. Each time we've moved something, there's been a moment of recollection, an elegiac pause in the day's passing.

But now, once and for all, I have to decide what to keep, what to let go. Will I keep all my mother-in-law's costume jewelry? The three Baroque hand-carved Italian chairs, a wedding gift from my husband's grandfather to his grandmother? My mother's clothing? My sister's handmade doll's dresses? My grandmother's rusted sieve, carried to America from Italy? My father-in-law's tools? And what of my grandparents' marriage licenses, visas, passports, birth certificates, naturalization papers, work permits, each item a small, irreplaceable piece of our family's history?

If I decide to get rid of any of these things, will I regret it? For once it's gone, I can never get it back: another piece of my family's past, obliterated by me. Going through these items makes me think about all the time that has vanished; it forces me to recognize what I often overlook: that time is fleeting and our lives are finite. They begin, we live them for the most part without cherishing their miracle and mystery, they end. Bumper sticker: *Wish I were here.*

As I go through my possessions, deciding what to pack, I become ashamed of all the stuff I have. I pride myself on my frugality, on buying only what I need, on turning leftovers into another meal. How lacking in self-knowledge I am.

But there are over two hundred cookbooks, scores of books I haven't yet read, bins of yarn, a stash of watercolors. As I survey all my stuff, I vow I'll never buy another book, hank of yarn, tube of paint.

What shocks me most is the pasta. Forty pounds of it: penne, bucatini, orecchiette, farfalle, spaghetti, croxetti—seemingly enough for a year. I tell myself I have bought all this pasta because as a child, I never had enough food because of my mother's erratic and eccentric cooking habits.

Packing makes me confront all my unrealized desires: the recipes I haven't tried; the sweaters I haven't knit; the books I haven't read; the watercolors I haven't painted; the photograph albums I haven't filled. It makes me see the "too-muchness" of my nature. Too many cookbooks, too much wool and pasta, too much, too much, too much. Is this because of my family's early history of poverty? Do I need all this stuff because my sense of self is tenuous and these objects remind me of what I want to do with my time?

I know that much of what I own will outlast me and that one day my sons will have to go through my possessions and decide what to keep, what to throw away, just as I must now, and that it will pain them as much as it now pains me. Perhaps they too will hang on to a few totemic objects for a while, then one day jettison them from their lives.

The day we move, I pack my car with my most precious possessions, everything I don't want to entrust to the movers. Thirty-five volumes of my writing journals. A framed photograph my husband's taken of me standing in front of the Dome on a trip to Paris when we were chasing Henry Miller's ghost. A few first editions of Virginia Woolf's novels. A stained glass lampshade made by my father. The ceramic pieces by my son Justin and by my sister. My son Jason's blown glass pieces and pastels. An herbal sampler embroidered by my mother. My hand-sewn quilt—five years of work, there. My most beloved knitted sweaters. A few pieces of my mother's and mother-in-law's heirloom jewelry. Boxes of family photographs. My grandkids' paintings—volcanoes and rockets, flowers and fish. A clock that my grandmother brought from Italy—I stopped the clock, wrapped it in towels, packed the winding key.

I have persuaded my husband it's better if I go ahead, if he deals with the movers. He knows I don't want to watch the house being dismantled, don't want to see it emptied. Can't bear to see the bed where I've read myself to sleep every night, where we've made love thousands of times, disassembled. Can't bear to see the desk where I've written my books wrapped up and carted away. Can't bear to see the kitchen stripped of all my cooking equipment—my "toys." Can't bear to watch the ornately carved antique wooden dining room table we'd bought at a junk shop for sixty dollars, wresting it away from someone who wanted to paint it white, broken down and wrapped in quilts. Can't bear to see our Mark Reichert painting, bought with money we didn't have when we were in our thirties, taken off the dining room wall where it has been silent witness to festive dinners too numerous to count. Can't bear to see my mother's gilded mirror taken off the living room wall where it had hung since soon after her death, when my father moved into his second wife's home and getting that mirror assuaged some of my grief; having it was like having a memorial to her, and each day as I passed it, I could remember my mother standing in front of it when I was little, patting her hair into place before going out, could remember her adjusting the veil on her hat the day of my wedding, could remember her gazing into it the day she went to the hospital the last time, saying, "Mildred, you look like the wrath of God."

And so I'm not there when the movers take all the furniture and boxes of books out of the house; not there when all the paintings come off the walls; not there when the rugs are rolled up; not there when my husband closes and locks the door to the house.

And so I don't see what I don't want to see and don't expect to ever see: the old house emptied of everything that has made it our home, the old house transformed from being our home into a place that has lost its soul.

On the day after our move, in my new house, I unwrap my grandmother's clock. After her death, it was given to my mother, and my mother had given it to my son Jason. But he's given it to me.

"It should have been yours instead of mine," Jason tells me. But my mother had a special affection for this grandson, one that transcended the usual bond most grandparents feel. I was the daughter she couldn't care for; he was the grandson who gave her joy.

I know I will put this clock on top of my mother's china closet, which became mine shortly after her death. My father calls me one day to tell me to come and get the china closet if I want it; otherwise he's going to call a hauler to get rid of it and everything else from our family's life together—furniture, photographs, memorabilia. My father is moving on to a new life with a new wife. His new home has no place for the china closet my mother and he bought when they moved to the suburbs after World War II, no place for my family's photos, none for my sister's pottery, my mother's embroidered samplers. "What a bastard," my husband says. And then we rent a U-Haul and collect everything.

I had stopped the clock at 1:14, just before wrapping and moving it. The clock face is a burnished bronze with ordinal numerals that my father had etched onto it when he refurbished it.

I am tired from the move. So when I take up the key to wind the clock, I drop it and the key skitters over to the heat register, drops into it far beyond the reach of any hand.

The key, irreplaceable. The clock, stopped, marking the moment when I left my old home behind to move to this new place.

PACKING THE REMAINS OF A LIFE . . .
During the Battle of Britain, Virginia Woolf experienced the difficult task of sorting through and packing a lifetime of possessions after a beloved home is severely damaged. Both Woolf's Tavistock Square home, which she was vacating, and her Mecklenburgh Square house, where she was moving, had been hit by bombs; Woolf's possessions, at the time of the bombing, were divided between the two. Although the Mecklenburgh Square home wasn't completely destroyed, all the windows were broken, and a second bomb explosion had caused more damage, making a "terrific mess," rendering the house uninhabitable. This left the Woolfs no home in London, and they traveled there from Rodmell to see what could be salvaged.

When they entered the Mecklenburgh Square flat, they discovered "mushrooms sprouting on the carpets, pools standing on the chairs, and glass to the right and left"; while they were there, a ceiling collapsed. "The passion of my life, that is the City of London—to see London all blasted," she wrote, "racked my heart." Her days became reduced to "fights with matter." The labor of packing made her "all black and blue." She tried not to "give into despair or rage" but to work steadily at what seemed to be the impossible job of salvaging what she could, cleaning, and packing. She boxed up letters and books, moved them to Rodmell.

It was difficult for her to be "surrounded by the melancholy relics" of her London life, and seeing them underscored that this blessed part of her life was over. Particularly painful was the sight of four tons of damaged books, many from her father's library. Objects she'd valued had become "impedimenta," giving her not pleasure but pain. There is no doubt that the experience of living through the consequences of the disaster of the bombing of London, the end of her beloved London way of life, the loss of her homes, the destruction of so many of her precious possessions, and the overwhelming work of packing, sorting, cleaning, and discarding contributed to the deep depression preceding her suicide.

FOUR

"Adrift"

Life After Moving

LIMINAL TIME . . .

A week after my husband and I move from our longtime home in Teaneck to a wonderful house, a restored Craftsman, in Montclair, New Jersey, I'm in a panic. It's a dream house with quartersawn oak beams in the living room, wooden floors, a sunny reading room, a wide and welcoming front porch. It's hard to believe it had once been derelict before it was rescued and restored by a team of artisans who recover homes that might otherwise be demolished. They create easy-to-care-for spaces with informal gathering places, and intimate recesses, and outdoor living areas—everything one could ever want.

Though I know how lucky I am, right after our move I'm blindsided by feelings of loss, sorrow, disorientation, emptiness. I feel that this house isn't home and never will be. I haven't anticipated these feelings, though I know moving is one of life's most stressful experiences, and they are incapacitating me. Sometimes I am even terrified, a feeling way out of proportion, I tell myself, to those normally arising from a move. Nothing bad has happened to me. This is a positive transition. I want these difficult feelings to go away, to get on with my life. But I'm not sure what my life will be in this new place.

John R. O'Neil's *The Paradox of Success* explains why this might be happening. Difficulty, he writes, is sometimes easier to endure than positive life transitions. When you're in trouble or having a hard time, friends and relatives are more likely to commiserate with you and help you. When you're experiencing what others regard as something positive, like moving to a beautifully restored home, no one wants to hear about your stress. Paradoxically, you can feel most isolated during life's sweetest moments.

This move is far from a hardship, yet it has made me feel *unsettled* and alone. Right after a move, normal life ceases. Liminal life—the life that is neither here nor there—begins. These difficult-to-live-through interstices, I've read, are necessary for growth: the psychic spaces where the old self is shed and the new one begins to develop. I knew how to live in the old place; I don't yet know how to live here. The old house felt filled with life, infused with memory; this house is an empty vessel and it's up to me to fill it with life, but I wonder what that life will be like. Still, the prospect of change allures me. This liminal time, though uncomfortable, is necessary for me to adapt.

But at times I don't want a new self, for it has taken me years to learn who that old self was and to live in a way that made serenity, which I've come to value above all things, possible. I liked my old self just fine the way she was, but she seems to have vanished. The person I was in the old house seems to have stayed there.

I miss my old house: the views out its windows—even of the derelict fence outside my study about which I often complained; the walk I took each morning to the other side of town, where the streets meandered in imitation of an English village; the bruised kitchen countertops where I'd cooked so many meals; the old living room that was my sanctuary. I feel as if I'm mourning. And I suppose I am.

I'm homesick and want the solace of home during this transitional time. I don't seem to know who I am or who I will become here. I feel rootless: all the touchstones of my life are gone and my comfortable, safe routine—walking and knitting in early morning, writing till noon, reading for the classes I'm teaching at Hunter College—has evaporated. I can't stick to a schedule and my life seems haphazard. I'm more tired than I've been since my children's infancy because of the physical labor of packing and unpacking, lifting heavy boxes, arranging and rearranging furniture.

What I'm feeling seems deeper than dislocation: it feels more primal, more terrifying, beyond the reach of language and explanation. All I can say is that I'm feeling as if I don't know who I am, that I've lost the self I was, that the real "me" has been left behind, the real "me" isn't living here but rather an impostor self I don't know. And I miss the real "me," want her back. But I'm afraid I've lost her for good. I remember reading about tribal rituals to find wandering souls and reunite them with their corporeal bodies. I wish I could undertake such a ritual, wish I could hear a wise person say, *Your spirit is wandering. It hasn't found you yet, but it will. Give it time and it will come back to you.*

THE ALLURE OF CHANGE . . .
A woman I met in a coffee shop in Montclair soon after I moved told me about how she had moved frequently and how she felt different in every place she lived. She'd lived in five places in the

past two years, and aside from the annoyance of changing addresses and banks and finding new doctors and all that, she told me that it didn't bother her at all; it energized her and changed her. She said she and her first husband had lived in a Victorian in Montclair that they'd fixed up. After the renovations were complete, their marriage fell apart. She moved with her kids into her parents' rent-controlled apartment in Greenwich Village while they spent the winter in Florida. She decided she didn't want to raise her kids in New York, so she moved to Hoboken. There she met a man and fell in love. They combined their families (together with dogs, cats, and turtles) in his house in Montclair. After a few months, they moved to another house, the house she'd just moved into when I met her.

When I asked how she'd managed all this change, all the packing and unpacking, and whether it had been unsettling, she shrugged and said, "Wherever you go, there you are." She talked about how she felt she carried "home" inside her and had never felt out of place no matter where she lived. Her strategy was to tell herself, *This is where I am right now.* Though unwinding her first marriage was wrenching, she told me she didn't mind leaving the house she'd shared with her first husband because she looked forward to moving.

To her, all this change was freeing and each new place exciting. She discovered different aspects of herself in each new place, and she found all the renewal invigorating. In her Montclair Victorian she'd felt secure and settled (until her marriage turned sour). In Greenwich Village, alive and excited. In Hoboken, comfortable and easygoing. And now back in Montclair, outgoing and companionable. And she believed the changes resulted from the places where she'd lived.

Marie Arana echoes this idea of how the psyche changes

depending on where you live in her memoir *American Chica.*
The book describes how her family moved from Cartavio to Paramonga in Peru. In Cartavio she had lived in what she called an
"inward-looking house" behind high walls. In Paramonga, though,
she lived right on the central boulevard unshielded from what
happened in the community beyond her home. In the first place
she was introverted; in the second, more outgoing. When her
family moved from Chile to Wyoming, she described the difference between her sense of rootedness in Chile and her sense of
expansiveness living under the big sky in Wyoming.

FITTING WORDS TO PLACE . . .

The day the Irish poet Eavan Boland packed the contents of her
flat in Dublin for a move to the suburbs, she became panic-
stricken. It occurred when she was packing her books into boxes.
Her poetry, she realized, had been nourished by her life in Dublin. What would become of her life and work as a poet in suburbia, a place she associated with the prosaic.

She had become a writer in Dublin. On her shelves were the
works of influential poets and writers. As she took her the books
off her shelves, she realized she'd become a poet *because* she'd
lived in this city: "Poetry was safe here . . . within this circle of li-
braries and pubs and talks about stanzas and cadences."

Packing made her realize she'd be leaving the site of her
inspiration and moving to a place where, as wife and mother,
she'd be living "a life unrecorded in the [poetic] tradition I had
inherited—in a suburb, with bus timetables and painted shelves
and school runs." She assumed life in the suburbs was unfit as
a subject for poetry, and she feared she would lose her calling.
She thought suburban women didn't write about their ordinary

existence and so she could no longer use her life as a subject for her art. This insight precipitated her crisis. Although she might be able to write poems, her "life would threaten to stay outside them."

In time Boland learned that her despair was rooted in her family's history of moves. She recalled a childhood memory of "moving vans, of adult voices late at night." When she was five, her family emigrated from Ireland to London: "One morning I was woken before dawn, dressed in a pink cardigan and skirt, put in a car, taken to an airport." Everything about her London life was different from her Irish life. She felt she'd belonged in Ireland; she loved the sight of flowers growing along a stone wall and the fields beyond. In London, "the Irish were unwelcome" and the streets felt hemmed-in to her. Reflecting on the disorientation of that time, she realized that what she'd felt was a sense of desolation, a "rare and virulent homesickness." Much of her disorientation was caused by losing a language to describe the sounds and sights of Ireland and her incapacity to formulate a language appropriate to speaking about her London life—precisely what she feared about moving to the suburbs as an adult: that she would lose her voice and become incapable of communicating her inner life and her experience in this new place. "I was adrift," she wrote, ". . . I could have been a character who had woken from a lyric fever in an old novel, unable to remember a name, a place of origin."

When she was fourteen, Boland's family moved back to Ireland, and she again became disoriented. Because she was now an émigré, she felt like an exile in her own country: she had "lost not only a place but the past that goes with it and, with it, the clues from which to construct a present self."

What saved her in childhood was her imagination. She began to write poetry and started finding words to describe where she was and who she was: she "started fitting words to place." She came to know the place she lived and the person she'd become by writing.

After Boland moved from Dublin to Dundrum, a suburb of Dublin, when she was married and in her twenties, she realized she could once again resolve this difficult juncture in her life by forcing herself to "reexamine modes of expression and poetic organization" to find new ones suitable to her suburban experience. Not content to keep her life separate from her art, Boland would have to refashion her poetry to render it capable of expressing her life in this new place.

Once she began to write poetry in the suburbs, she came to realize that suburban life was as significant as city life. Suburban lives were "mythic, not because of their strangeness but because of their powerful ordinariness." The suburbs were constantly changing: nothing stayed the same for long—new houses were constructed in fields, old neighbors moved out, and new people moved in. Here her subject matter would have to deal with "the coming loss" all who lived there must endure. Paradoxically, this was how she found a sense of permanence in both her life and her work—by realizing and writing about the fact that change is the only permanent thing in life.

The effects of moving are experienced in the body, in the imagination, in the realm of desire. What the eye sees, what the body feels, what the heart yearns for, what remains and what has been lost—these are difficult at first to describe. As skilled a writer as J. M. Coetzee discovered that he struggled to find words to properly convey what he felt when he moved from South Africa to London in the 1960s, when he was in his twenties. He describes this crisis in his memoir *Youth,* written in the third person to allow the distance he felt necessary to relate his experience. He found he could not immediately plumb the consequences of this move on the formation of his character, its impact on his work. Nor could he contextualize his experience in the history of the time. At first he felt adrift. It took time, reflection, and writing to understand.

Coetzee moved to escape his family—his mother's excessive coddling, his father's failures—but he also moved because he believed South Africa was headed toward revolution and because he imagined London would be an ideal place to work. Once there, though, he felt he was fighting for his life. He was miserable; he had panic attacks. Though he knew his writing was his lifeline, he still couldn't work; days passed, he says, "in a fog of grey exhaustion."

Coetzee believed the poetry he'd written in South Africa was far superior to the trivial poems he'd started in London. So he turned to prose, but found he couldn't write about South Africa because he was no longer there. Nor could he write about London, because he didn't know it well enough and he feared his outsider's view would put him at a disadvantage. "He has not mastered London," he writes in *Youth.* "If there is any mastering going on, it is London mastering him."

Coetzee believed he was initially scarred by his move. "South Africa," he writes, "is a wound within him. How much longer before the wound stops bleeding." Initially, writing about his move pained him; his encounters with the blank page left him in despair. In time, though, he found the form and language appropriate to writing about South Africa, sometimes using the persona of an aging white South African, as in his novels *Disgrace* and *Waiting for the Barbarians.*

MOVING, A KIND OF DEATH . . .

The night before our move, I have a dream. In the dream, I awaken in an unfamiliar room. I have just moved, and there are boxes that I'll have to unpack all around my bed. I am sleeping on a small cot, like the one in my parents' Hoboken tenement. The room is tiny, windowless, tucked under a stairwell. My grandmother stands in the kitchen next to this tiny space. Someone—I can't see who—asks her where I've gone. She responds in Italian, "Se ne sono andata." She moved on.

The walls of the tiny room are covered with newspaper photographs of men at war, clambering through water, their rifles aloft; of houses blown apart by bombs. On the wall is a placard reading, "Why all this sorrow? The child stands in front of the window, and beyond, is history."

When I awaken, I wonder what the dream means. How can I associate these tragedies with my own experience? Why should this move elicit this dream? And then I remember my first move as a young child during wartime. My father away in the Pacific; my mother afraid each day will be the day when the telegram arrives announcing my father's death; her father moving us to a safer apartment next to his; the newspapers documenting the war displayed each day on a rack in the drugstore next to where we live. I don't yet know the reason for the move. But all my life, remembering that move terrifies me. Each move we make, it seems, recalls all the moves we've made before.

I search through books for the source of the quotation in my dream. And find it in Virginia Woolf's *Jacob's Room*. Jacob Flanders, who will die during World War I, is sitting in a sailboat with his friend Timmy Durrant. Jacob looks back and sees smoke pluming from the chimneys of cottages on shore. He thinks there is something "infernally sad" about these dwelling places, although they seem to connote safety, shelter, even coziness. When we are children, he thinks, "We start transparent, and then the cloud thickens. All history backs our pane of glass. To escape is vain."

All history backs our pane of glass. No home is insulated from the world, as my childhood homes weren't. The windows of every home open to the outside world, where history unfolds, unstoppable, impinging on the lives of those within. Perhaps that's where my feelings during my move to Montclair originate: in that first move during that long and terrible war. Perhaps I'm feeling so vulnerable because I recognize what I so often forget: that no home, no matter how beloved, assures us of permanent safety.

And, too, there was the way my grandmother talked about moving. When she spoke to me about leaving the South of Italy and coming to America to marry my grandfather, she would say, "Me ne sono andata," meaning "I got out of there; I moved on." But when she spoke to me about dying, she would also say, "Se ne sono andati": they moved on. So from a very early age, there it was, dying and moving, all tangled together.

And moving *is* a kind of death. For we must let go of a place, though we may not want to, and of the spaces that have held special significance for us, though, being human, we have no doubt taken them for granted: the living room that felt just right when we sat in it; the east-facing bedroom that bathed us in early-morning sunshine; the little garden on the side of the house where we had our breakfast on warm summer days. We must often let go of friends: the next-door neighbor who watched our children; the neighbor who brought muffins; the kids who rumbled up and down the street. They all die into memory, remaining, always, the people they were. And we let go, too, of the person we used to be in that place, even as we cannot quite believe how mutable we are.

Someone else now lives in the house I thought I'd never leave. And the life I've lived in that house, I now speak of in the past tense, *When we lived in Teaneck*, instead of in the present: *We live in Teaneck*. And this simple shift of tense marks the fact of *time passing—* something I wasn't as aware of in quite this way until I moved.

I have closed a door behind me. The keys now belong to someone else. I can't open that door anymore, and the place beyond it is now as inaccessible to me as all the life I've lived there, retrievable only in photographs, story, and memory. Still, while I lived in that house it seemed that my life would continue there forever, that it was as substantial as the sofa I settled into in my study with a cup of tea at the end of each day.

Once, when I was very small, when my grandmother spoke to me of moving, she walked into her bedroom, rummaged through her drawers, and picked out my grandfather's old neckerchief, a safety pin rusty with age, a bead that had fallen off her daily rosary, and a little cross fashioned from Easter Sunday palm, and took all these treasures into the kitchen. She spread out the neckerchief, placed the pin, the bead, the cross within, topped them with a fennel biscotti, pulled the corners of the neckerchief up and over, and tied a neat bundle. "Here, poveretta, my poor little one," she said handing me the package, "now you are ready to move on."

QUIET AND HAPPY FOR THE FIRST TIME . . .
In the early part of 1905, after her father's death, twenty-two-year-old Virginia Stephen (later, Woolf) moved from her family home

at 22 Hyde Park Gate to a new home at 46 Gordon Square in Bloomsbury, which she shared with her siblings. She immediately instituted a daily ritual—writing, walking to explore her new neighborhood, beautifying her home—which made her feel more at home and less unsettled. Routine was a force that insulated her, she knew, against the perils that might come with change.

Even before her belongings were in place, after this move and throughout her life, she implemented her daily writing routine, taking up a work in progress or often beginning something new. She experimented with other ways of working, acknowledging that moving might bring change to her writing. Writing helped Woolf feel centered and secure, so she knew it was necessary to begin working immediately after moving and not wait to feel settled.

During transitions she often grounded herself by reviewing her family and personal history in her journal, taking stock of her life, of what remained and what had changed. She wrote too about her new surroundings and planned for the alterations that would make wherever she was living more beautiful or her life there more comfortable; her plans always included outfitting a private place for work and contemplation. She pondered where she would place her cherished possessions, which gave her a needed sense of continuity; made lists of what she needed to purchase; planned shopping expeditions to find items she needed.

She would usually write from ten to one, except Sunday and holidays. Afternoons, she would take a pleasurable excursion: a walk in the park; lunch with relatives or friends; a visit to an art exhibit, an old bookshop, or a library. Late afternoons she'd return home to fix up her rooms or read a book or type her handwritten morning's work or write a journal entry. Evenings she would again read or write letters or pay bills or listen to music, or late in her life, play bowls. Or she might go to the theater or a concert, or out to visit friends. She believed in living a balanced life, taking up her work, physical exercise, social life, and private pleasure, each in its turn, daily. Hers was not a cloistered life of obsessive work; she had learned that working too hard was dangerous and that not working at all was equally risky. In addition to writing daily, she needed a plan, needed to know what to do when; without this, she felt adrift. During moves, she felt this need even more acutely.

Before moving from Hyde Park Gate to Gordon Square, Woolf had begun work on a biographical piece about her father, a work she continued just after her move. She also undertook two new challenges: translating selections from Thucydides and teaching history once a week to workingwomen at Morley College.

Before her move, Woolf had published book reviews in the Women's Supplement of the *Guardian,* and she'd sent preliminary drafts to friends for criticism. After, she decided to allow only editors to review her work, marking a significant shift in her sense of herself as a writer, from that of a talented amateur to a professional. She now had a room of her own to write in where she wouldn't be interrupted and could think long and hard about what was best for her. Inhabiting the new space also prompted a change in self-definition: she no longer saw herself as merely the youngest daughter in a famous family and began to take her work seriously. Her room became a place where, she said, "I can shut myself up, and see no one, and read myself into peace."

Her move was a major transition. She had recently recovered from a breakdown after her father's death, a breakdown caused in part by her half brothers' sexual abuse. The move to Gordon Square away from the site of trauma signified to her that her "horrible long illness" was behind her. Still, she did not bury the past but reviewed her life to ease her transition. She wrote about the excitement of beginning an independent life and her hopes for the future. As she wrote to her friend Violet Dickinson, "You can't think what an exquisite joy every minute of my life is to me now, and my only prayer is that I might live to be 70."

She thought about the characteristics of her family home at Hyde Park Gate, contrasting them with those of her new home. She analyzed how these different living spaces affected her life and her psyche. Her former home had been furnished by her mother, Julia Stephen, in typical Victorian fashion. No light entered the house; the windows were covered with heavy draperies, making the interiors dark, gloomy, and, Woolf thought, extremely depressing. The furniture was upholstered in red velvet and the woodwork was painted black, making the house funereal and suffocating. She wondered whether the architecture of that house—her room and her half brothers' were far away from her parents'—permitted her half brothers to abuse her without parental interference.

Woolf reveled in the atmosphere of the Gordon Square home. Her sister Vanessa had decorated it in a way that was bright, light, airy, and sparsely furnished. No draperies blocked the drawing room window and Woolf could look out into the trees in the square. Here her spirit soared. "The light and air after the rich red gloom of Hyde Park Gate," she wrote, "were a revelation."

But there was far more noise here—an "interminable roar & rattle & confusion of wheels & voices." Woolf was extremely sensitive to noise and deeply missed the quiet of her old home. Still, the sounds in Gordon Square made Woolf feel energized, and she began to accept it as an outward manifestation of her newfound engagement with London's bustle.

Woolf also missed her old walks in Kensington Gardens, near Hyde Park Gate, which held more charm for her than Regent's Park near Gordon Square. Regent's Park had only "flat open stretches of grass, where you never lose sight of houses." But she turned what might have been a disadvantage into an asset and planned her walks through Bloomsbury's streets, discovering that street life here was "far more interesting" than in her old neighborhood. "Streetwalking" became a wonderful new habit that lasted a lifetime, helping to forge her passion for the city, satisfy her immense curiosity, and provide subjects and characters for essays and novels.

Woolf loved organizing and decorating her bedroom and sitting room. She understood that this was the simplest way to get over her feelings of dislocation: making a place your own. She arranged her bedroom furniture; hung paintings, family portraits, and autographed letters from famous people; bought flowers; found the perfect spot to display each housewarming gift— including a "huge china inkpot" from her friend Violet Dickinson. Objects that evidenced her family's prominence in literary and artistic circles gave her a sense of pride and continuity with the past. She bought a mirror for the space over her writing table to "liven up the room," but she also understood its symbolic significance: at Hyde Park she hated looking into mirrors, but here she was seeing herself anew. She placed her "beloved leather backed books" onto shelves; outfitted her study's fireplace with wrought-iron fire irons and a beaten brass coal scuttle; bought an "extravagant little table"; and surrounded herself with "a huge mass of manuscripts and letters and proof-sheets and pens and inks," all marks of her profession—these she would tidy from time to time, but they eventually would once again become "a happy frenzy of litter." Having spent more than she thought she should, she resolved to write articles to make money to pay for the extravagant luxuries she bought to beautify her rooms.

Once her rooms were arranged to suit her, she realized how much the move had improved her quality of life. "I am feeling really quiet and happy and able to stretch my legs out on a sofa for the first time for 7 months," she wrote. "The house is a dream of loveliness."

On March 1, 1905, Virginia and her siblings threw a housewarming party to introduce their friends and relations to their new home. The days before the party were filled with work (securing china, borrowing silver, ordering food and drink) and the day of the party was filled with anxiety and more work (rearranging furniture, arranging flowers in vases, picking up refreshments). The party was a celebration of Woolf and her siblings' passage into adulthood, of their newly independent life. It lasted until well after midnight. Although during the celebration there were "moments of difficulty," Woolf believed it had been successful housewarming—an important way station in settling into a home.

But the next morning, as usual, though she felt lazy, it was back to her routine. On this day, Woolf translated portions of Aristotle's *Poetics*. The work was difficult, but it was accomplished within the sanctity of her own room in her own home.

FIVE

"A Space for the Psyche's Hinterland"

Homemaking

WORK OF THE SPIRIT . . .

After we move, I tell myself I can postpone any task to sit and read and sip a cup of tea, as I'd imagined myself doing when I first saw this house, so that I can truly begin to live here. But weeks after I still feel compelled to work nonstop to make this house feel like our home. I force myself to accomplish items on a "to do" list, moving from one task to another, yearning to sit in the living room, yearning to take a long hot bath, yearning to set a beautiful table for supper.

Perhaps I'm working so hard to blunt my sense of loss and displacement. Perhaps, too, I'm washing, ironing, and storing away every last napkin, dusting every piece of pottery, polishing every piece of furniture to turn this into a perfect house, as if these tasks in and of themselves will accomplish this transformation. A Zen saying comes to my mind: "How you do one thing is how you do everything." How true this is, especially when it comes to homemaking, which, after all, is one important expression of a person's innermost self. This house won't change me unless I change myself, unless I permit myself time to relax and enjoy myself instead of working incessantly.

My husband, Ernie, is different. He's the kind of person who feels at home anywhere—in a grotty hotel room, in someone's guest room, and by the end of the first day, in each of the places we've moved. He doesn't look back, doesn't miss where we've lived before. He can live in the middle of the mess of moving, willing to plunk himself down anywhere to eat a store-bought meal. He'll sleep in a bed without linen, rouse himself in time for work, shower (or take a sponge bath if we can't find the towels), dress, drink some awful coffee at a local diner, and go about his business on the day after a move as if he's lived there all his life. For him, there are no difficult transitions, and when I ask him why it's hard for me and not for him, he says he's never thought there was anything missing in his life so he's never thought that moving would change him.

I grumble about his nonchalance even as I envy it. Because I've been working so hard to set the house to rights, I've not done what I know I need to do to make this house a place where *I* feel at home.

It takes me weeks to realize that if I want to feel at home here I must establish a routine, perhaps not the same one as before, but one more suited to the life I want to create, with time for work, writing, self-care, and my family, yes, but also more time for cooking, knitting, excursions, and sustaining friendships than before. Routine—antidote to chaos, anchor in a transitional time, as I've learned from Virginia Woolf. I've been waiting to "settle in" before I start writing. But writing will help me "settle in."

I can make this house my home by doing the work of the

spirit here, doing my work with a Zen-like respect for the sacred-
ness of everyday life. Organizing a closet, polishing a desk, studying, writing, cooking, knitting, meditating, whatever—I've been
working mechanically and rushing through tasks to get them
done without reverence or attention. But to consecrate this house,
I must move more slowly, take my time. Only a shift in my relationship to time can make this home; only if I take my time will I
ever feel what the writer Mark Doty has called the "blossoming
[that] the work of homemaking might engender."

Although I've filled our house with precious objects—those
my family has made, some new carpets, freshly upholstered
chairs—I haven't yet filled it with myself, with those special acts
of attention that will breath soulfulness into it.

BUILDING IS WHAT I WILL DO . . .
Carl Jung's memoir, *Memories, Dreams, Reflections*, describes
how he built a house for himself in Bollingen on Zurich's upper
lake. Jung had been mesmerized by water since a childhood visit
to Germany's Lake Constance with his mother and "could not be
dragged away" from it. He loved the waves that washed upon the
shore, the glistening of sunlight on the water, the vast expanse of
a lake. When he was very young, he told himself that one day he
would live near a lake. "Without water," he thought, "nobody
could live at all."

As a grown man, Jung played childhood games, building
tiny structures from whatever washed up on shore in front of his
lakeside Zurich home. Between 1914 and 1917 he was in the midst
of confronting his "terrible inner world," distressed by "bizarre
images" from his unconscious. He couldn't read or write, so he
began the "conscious occupation of setting aside time each day

for children's play," hoping it would help him. "Building! This is what I'll do," he vowed.

During his prescribed playtime after lunch, he fashioned "little villages," "churches, houses, and castles surround[ing] stone squares," "rivers and canals." Once on impulse he used a red pebble as a "stone altar" within a little church he'd constructed. This unlocked the memory of a "dream of an underground phallus" that had terrified him as a child. He realized that his play was a ritual connected to his personal mythology and that he now had to examine what this mythology was. He knew that the idea of home and that building and furnishing a home were also connected to one's personal mythology, an understanding of which was necessary to lead a fulfilling life.

This insight became the foundation of his work with patients. He began to listen for the personal mythology embedded in his patients' stories during their treatment even as he thought about his own. "Building!" he wrote, "that was the beginning."

By 1922 Jung had stopped building childlike structures and began constructing a dwelling place for himself by hand. He suspected that this work would contribute greatly to understanding his psyche. Jung said that the house would become a "representation in stone of my innermost thoughts and of the knowledge I had acquired."

At first Jung planned a round "primitive one-story dwelling," a "wide, single-story tower" with a "hearth in the center and bunks along the wall." It evoked a kind of "African hut where the fire, ringed by a few stones, burns in the middle, and the whole life of the family revolves around this center." It would be an image of "familial wholeness."

By 1923, the first edifice—the round house—was built. Jung

believed it to be a "suitable dwelling tower." There he felt a powerful sense of "repose and renewal." In time, Jung realized something was still lacking. The house, he said, "did not yet express everything that needed saying." He realized his building reflected the evolution in his thinking about the archetypal meaning of home and its significance and how these related to his own personal mythology.

In 1927—now with the help of professional builders—Jung added a "central structure" with "a tower-like annex." It became "connected with the dead," especially the death of his mother in 1923. But it was also connected with "maturation" and rebirth. He felt that entering it was like reentering "a maternal womb" that would nourish him so he could become "what I was, what I am and what I will be." Death, rebirth—the necessary connections between them emerged as he contemplated the making of his home. When he was at the lakeside home, he felt life's difficulties lessen. And for a while he was satisfied.

Four years later, he again began to feel the structure was incomplete. So in 1931 he extended the house to include yet another "tower-like annex" because he wanted a room that could be entirely his, where, as he said, "I could exist for myself alone." He wanted this structure to be a private area for meditation and spiritual practice. Solitude became as necessary as communal life. This room, the most central and highest room, became Jung's private bedroom and study. He positioned his desk beneath a window overlooking the lake. He allowed no one into it without his permission; he locked the door and always carried the key with him as a talisman. Throughout the rest of his life, Jung would add carvings and paintings to the walls of this room to express what he'd learned during meditation. He would sometimes write sayings or quoted passages from his reading on the wall so that he was surrounded by his learning and insights, the history of his thought process.

In 1935, again dissatisfied, Jung felt he needed a space that was fenced in but also "open to the sky and to nature." He added a wall and made "a courtyard and a loggia by the lake": a place that manifested his connection with nature but that was nonetheless protected and constructed by him seemed necessary.

When he reflected on why he had made these changes, Jung realized he'd been compelled to make them: he was responding to intuitions, to innermost needs. Over twelve years, he'd constructed a "quaternity"—four separate spaces, each representing one aspect of his evolving personal mythology, each satisfying some lack.

In 1955, after Jung's wife died, he realized that "the small central section which crouched so low, so hidden was myself!" After this discovery, he added an upper story, knowing it represented "myself, or my ego-personality." He knew he never could have done this as a younger man, for it would have seemed too presumptuous. But as an older man, it signified the "extension of consciousness" he'd achieved through hard work.

Jung learned that transforming a dwelling place can often accompany profound psychic changes but can also prompt them. Yielding to the impulse to build, transform, and embellish a living space can help us discover our innermost needs at any given time and the generative core at the nature of the self. Taken together, Jung's structures represented "a concretization of the individuation process," which he wasn't aware of as he built them. Only after the entire structure was finished did he understand that its seemingly accidental form had a profound integrity corresponding to his own evolving personal mythology. He learned that when people make changes in their home, they might be striving to bring their home into closer alignment with their changing personal mythologies and that meditating on these changes could reveal much.

Jung's detailed analysis of his work building the Bollingen house reveals how deeply significant homemaking can be in moving toward what he called "psychic wholeness" and in fashioning a place where we can be most deeply and authentically ourselves. But the creation of this kind of home must be reflective and ongoing and it must respond to deeply felt impulses, as Jung learned. "Here," Jung said, referring to Bollingen, "everything has its history, and mine; here is space for the spaceless kingdom of the world's and the psyche's hinterland."

A HOUSE OF MEMORY . . .

In 1958, Marguerite Duras bought a house in Neauphle-le-Château. When she saw the garden, she thought, "Yes, I would buy the house," and bought it "then and there." She was searching for a place where she could enjoy the solitude she believed was necessary for her to write in a new way.

As a girl, Duras lived in French Indochina. Her mother was alcoholic and, along with one of her brothers, was violent. Duras would escape from the chaos and danger of her family home and venture into "the green immensity of the jungle" nearby, where one could hear "the muffled cries of animals." There, paradoxically, Duras felt safe and at home. Throughout her life Duras had always sought "refuge in wild, foreign places," so she knew the garden with its ancient trees behind the house in Neauphle-le-Château would fill an important need.

It took two years of living there and organizing the house to suit her for Duras's "life with it" to really begin. She repainted it; she furnished rooms "using vestiges from the past . . . , cottons, silks, embroideries as old as the century, bouquets of wilted hydrangea, turn-of-the-century furniture, sideboards, cherrywood tables with molded legs." Though her childhood had been painful, she bought rattan cane chairs that reminded her of those on the terrace of her childhood home, where her mother would sit and "contemplate the sky, the mountains, the Mekong." She placed "cashmere shawls" and "threadbare rugs" about the rooms; arranged objects she found on her walks—"colocynths, pebbles"— on the surfaces of her tables. She hung paintings and arranged her books and screenplays on shelves to remind herself of past accomplishments when she believed she might never again write. She aimed for the decorative effect of her home as a work in progress, a reminder that her life in this house would be ever-changing, not static.

Duras positioned an old mirror left behind by the previous owner where she would encounter it each day to remind herself of the house's past and provide a link with its history. Seeing the mirror, she would imagine the private lives and stories of past inhabitants, whom she had become connected with simply by living here. She sought to become integrated into the life of this house. Her time here, she knew, was limited, just as theirs had been. Any house, Duras believed, is a house of memory, a house that revives childhood memories and contains memories "accumulated over centuries, in the obscure mystery of places." Although a house may be ours for a time, it belongs, still, to its former inhabitants and to history, for it contains everything anyone who inhabited it experienced there—pleasure and pain, loneliness, passion, desire, fulfillment, frustration, consummation, expectation.

Duras's book *Writing* explains the relationship between her life in this house and the evolution of her creative work. "One does not find solitude, one creates it," she says, by spending long periods alone in a house. Immediately following a move is a difficult time because we must face the inevitable fear that encountering a house on its own terms entails. When we are home alone—and here Duras speaks of what she believes to be universally true—we will often feel a primal terror. But we can love a house only after we experience this and learn to endure it.

For Duras, though, solitude could also be dangerous; it also meant "the solitude of alcohol." Three times while living at Neauphle-le-Château, Duras "went to the edge."

Duras describes how loss became the subject of her work in novels like *The Ravishing of Lol Stein* and *The Vice-Consul* at Neauphle-le-Château because moving inevitably involves loss. New houses often invite us to recall the houses of our past, the homes we have lost. Duras's family was forced to leave their home in Prey Nop, Cambodia, on the edge of the China Sea, in 1932, when Duras was eighteen, because the land was ruined by floods. The pain of leaving remained with her throughout her life, and that period in her life became the subject of much of her mature work. Any move she made in adulthood awakened childhood feelings of loss and displacement.

Her novel *The Sea Wall*, written before her move—she used the money from the film rights to buy the house—describes her mother's move to French Indochina and subsequent purchase of that home on the sea. Duras's mother moved there because she was sick of village life in northern France; she succumbed to propaganda luring young people to the colonies, promising a fortune would await them there. Duras's father and mother signed up to become teachers. In time, her disillusioned father went back to

France, eventually dying there without returning to the family. But her mother stayed on with the three children born there.

Duras's mother saved money for ten years to purchase land near the China Sea. She built a bungalow and hired two hundred laborers to erect a sea wall so she could cultivate the land. But the wall "collapsed like a house of cards, in one single night, spectacularly, succumbing to the elemental and implacable onslaught" of the sea, drowning all the crops. Duras's mother realized she had been duped into buying worthless land by colonial officials; they made fortunes selling it to naive colonials, then reclaiming it and reselling it to the next victim. Her mother had been swindled out of her life savings.

Though she tried, her mother was unable to reclaim the money she lost, and as a result, according to Duras, went mad—although her alcoholism surely contributed. When she saw her three children enjoying themselves swimming, roaming the land unfettered and free, she berated them. Duras and her younger brother became the victims of her violent rage. Their older brother also attacked her and her brother while their mother looked on, unaffected, perhaps even enjoying the spectacle—Duras wrote these scenes into her novel *The North China Lover*.

In *Writing*, Duras suggests that recalling pain experienced in our childhood and mourning our lost innocence are necessary if we are to develop a fulfilling life in our adult homes. Confronting pain and loss is necessary if we are to break the bonds of old habits and reinvent ourselves or create an authentic work of art in a new place. First, Duras writes, you must "find yourself . . . at the bottom of a hole" and feel "a vast emptiness" before you can search for what it will take to fill it. You must lose yourself in order to find yourself again.

For Duras, moving recalled not only her childhood but also

humanity's past. Relocating from a familiar place to a new place was always risky, terrifying, and dangerous for our ancient ancestors. This is why moving inevitably awakens "a savage state . . . as ancient as time" within us: these feelings seem hardwired in the human psyche, a relic of our ancient past. Moving unleashes fear, yes, but it also provides as compensation the potential for boldness, bravery, and newfound strength, necessary characteristics to cultivate if our species is to survive and we ourselves are to flourish.

Buying the house at Neauphle-le-Château was healing for Duras. It consoled her for her childhood pain. In purchasing it, she did "something important for myself, something definitive." Here "a certain window, a certain table" "populated" her life and "made it magic," rendering meaning to the life she lived there.

Writing—"habits of black ink"—consecrated this house. She said she "finally had a house" where she "could hide in order to write books." The emptiness Duras first felt after buying the home at Neauphle-le-Château became filled by thoughts of "a possible book." She began a period of "naked writing, like something . . . terrible to overcome." Without this difficult period of adjustment, she believed she might have written only facile, charming, inauthentic books—"books . . . for whiling away the hours," not "books that become embedded in one's thoughts and toll the black mourning for all life."

In time this became "the house of writing" for Duras. She believed the books she wrote there depended on *this particular* house—the light flooding the house from the garden, the table she sat at to write, the light "reflecting off the pond." And she included it in her work: the rosebush outside the window of her room appeared in *The Atlantic Man*, a narrative about a former lover.

At first she wrote in the mornings without any firm schedule on the second floor. Then later in time she began to write in the living room on the ground floor, where she could see the garden. And she wrote well—*Moderato Cantabile*, the book that marked "a complete break" with her previous work; *The Ravishing of Lol Stein*, about a love triangle; *The Vice-Consul*, about a young Vietnamese girl rejected by her mother after becoming pregnant. Each was about "the force of destiny"; each took the shape of "a Racinian tragedy." Because of living here, Duras developed hallmarks of her mature style—"interrupting the normal progression of the narrative, short-circuiting it with baffling parenthetical sequences"—learned, in part, from her study of Marcel Proust's work.

Some time after Duras began living in Neauphle-le-Château, she witnessed a mundane event she believed was dense with meaning. As she awaited the arrival of a friend, she became aware of a common fly on a wall in the final moments of its life. She "leaned closer to watch it die," curious about what dying looks like.

The fly took a long time to die, ten or fifteen minutes, and she watched it struggle "against death." But she could not continue and left because she believed witnessing its death would be disrespectful, rendering it "even more horrible."

When her friend came, Duras told her what had transpired and her friend laughed at her concern. But Duras countered that the "death of a fly is still death" and decided to write about it. In contemplating the significance of the fly's death and her reaction to it and memorializing it, Duras realized that this encounter had solidified her connection with this house. A house "needs time around it, people, histories, 'turning points,' things like marriage, or the death of that fly, death, banal death—the death of one and the many at the same time" to become a home. For our lives within any house to become meaningful, Duras believed, we must respect the lives of all those who die while we live in that home. Contemplating life's tragedies and its inescapable transience forces us into an awareness of what home really means and into appreciating its sanctity.

And so Duras began keeping dead flowers around her as reminders of the passage of time and all that she'd lost in her life, all she could lose. "We never throw out flowers in this house," she wrote. "There are some rose petals that have been in a jar for forty years." We can learn that life is precious only if we remember that it will end one day, that all living things die. When we acknowledge our mortality, then our houses will truly become our homes.

HERE IN MY CORNER . . .

The painter Pierre Bonnard and his wife, Marthe, moved into a house at Le Cannet in Provence in the south of France on September 27, 1927. It is easy to see why Bonnard loved the place. Although the house was a simple two-story structure with a pitched roof, its setting was magnificent. It commanded "a stupendous view over Cannes, the bay, the Golfe de la Napoule and the mountains of the Esterel." The property had tiered stone walls and two reservoirs, and was bordered by a path alongside the Canal de la Siagne. Everywhere you looked, there was "an ever-changing spectacle, breathtaking in scope . . . with [c]ypresses stick[ing] up at intervals like dark vegetal columns silhouetted against the crystalline sky." Bonnard came here not because of the light—the reason given by many painters for moving south—but because of the colors in this magnificent landscape. The move to Le Cannet so shocked his sensibility that he painted as he never had before;

once there, he changed his relationship to color, his "palette became brighter, his compositions bolder and more simplified," as the critic Nicholas Watkins has said.

Bonnard enlarged the house, installing French windows in every room large enough to frame the views beyond, opening the house to nature. Regarding the view was integral to his life there — seeing the stony path behind the house leading to the Canal de la Siagne, the red roofs of the village itself tumbling down toward Cannes, the shape of the Esterel mountains outlined against the sea. Windows in Bonnard's painting came to signify that a house was a place both of "refuge" and also of "confinement," that our response to the rooms we inhabit vacillates between feelings of repose and restlessness, and that these poles of human experience must be represented on canvas.

Bonnard himself—not Marthe, who was so often lost in depression—was the architect of the house's changes. He had its facade painted "pink roughcast" and the shutters a light gray-green. He had walls torn down between two rooms on the ground floor to fashion it into the enlarged, oft-painted dining room. He installed electricity, central heating, running water. He built himself a small studio on the house's north-facing side to catch the light ideal for painting. He had the walls in the bedrooms painted blue; the outside of the cupboards, white; the interiors of the cupboards, red. He had the walls in the dining room, the small sitting room, and Marthe's bedroom painted a shade of yellow called "Naples." He furnished the rooms with simple wicker furniture and adorned tables with ceramic vases and Provençal terra-cotta pots made nearby. He decorated the bathroom where Marthe spent so much time bathing with gray-blue glazed tiles. When he planned the pattern of tiles behind the claw-foot tub where

Marthe bathed, can he have known he would spend so much of his artistic life painting her submerged in water and in sadness?

In making these changes, Bonnard was guided by Japanese aesthetic principals. He was a member of the group of artists called the Nabis—Hebrew for "the prophets"—and was known as "the very Japanese Nabi" because he studied Japanese art, which profoundly influenced his work. His home, too, reflected the Zen qualities of *wabi, sabi, shibui*—austerity, elegant simplicity, tastefulness.

Once settled in his house, Bonnard made paintings of each of its rooms, the view through its windows, its exterior, the garden, and the sights he encountered on his walks, over and over again. His evolving relationship to this house and its environs became the subject of his work. His home became the subject of meditation and contemplation; his best paintings, I believe, express the Zen qualities of *yugen*, a profound connection to a place, and *seijaku*, the stillness, quiet, and tranquility we experience in a place where we truly feel at home and which can only come with time and meditation. Bonnard's paintings show us how developing such a relationship to a home can become a deep spiritual practice. The work of Bonnard's lifetime at Le Cannet became "doing nothing but looking around him and within himself." So deep was his connection to Le Cannet that during World War II when his friend Henri Matisse suggested a move into a hotel where life would be far easier, Bonnard responded: "I assure you I'm much better here in my corner."

Each morning before painting, Bonnard took a walk for inspiration, to rediscover nature. He walked through the hills above his house, along the canal, through the olive, orange, and almond groves. He sketched and made a note of the weather. He wrote

Matisse that during his morning walks, he amused himself "by defining different conceptions of landscape—landscape as 'space,' intimate landscape, decorative landscape, etc." Though he might take the same walk each day, each day he would "see things differently . . . , the sky, objects, everything changes continually, you can drown in it." The only constant, he learned, was change.

These humble tasks—decorating a home, taking walks, painting—because they involved acts of attention on the part of Bonnard, became spiritual tasks. His life, his work, plumbed the mystery behind the simplest aspects of human existence. Making a home, apprehending it, contemplating it, appreciating it, realizing the abiding meaning behind its superficial appearance, as Bonnard demonstrated, can become something like a form of worship, a connection to something beyond ourselves, a way to approach the divine.

From reading books about Bonnard, I learned that his paintings were not created in situ—neither in the garden outside nor in the rooms of the house—but in his studio. He painted the *memory* of what he'd seen outside, of the rooms he inhabited. The dining room, often painted with a red cloth atop a table, sometimes with vases of flowers held too long in water, or bowls of overripe fruit. Marthe's small sitting room, its table cluttered with the detritus of a meal, its window often open to the view beyond, its walls sometimes acid yellow, sometimes all cool shadows. The bedroom, its little window overlooking a vague structure in the garden, and trees, and hills. And, of course, the bathroom, with the bathtub where Marthe spent so much of her time, bathing, bathing, bathing, always bathing, as if in bathing she could wash away the demons of her illness that made this house a place of sorrow too. In his studio, away from his subjects, Bonnard transformed the perfectly ordinary into the sublime.

The paintings often took years to complete, if in fact they ever were completed, for Bonnard had a habit of adding a daub of paint here or there years after he had declared them finished. His paintings took so long because he was painting not the appearance of things, but their essence: the essence of ordinary things revealed through their appearances. He was painting that Buddhist moment of enlightenment, called *aware* in Japanese, that comes only after much time, patience, hard work, and discipline, that moment when we see the familiar as if for the first time.

Bonnard once said, "I'm trying to do what I have *never* done: give the impression one has on entering a room: one sees everything and at the same time nothing." He wanted to "draw the spectator into the painting on a contemplative journey, in which familiar objects are encountered as though for the first time, forming unexpected relationships and meanings, and generating in the process a consciousness of the complexity of the experience that constitutes awareness on entering a room." Seeing a Bonnard painting invites us to transfer his vision to how we react and respond to the familiar places where we live. It is only familiarity, he seems to say, that can elicit such a profound relationship to our living spaces, but only if we see these places as if for the first time. But Bonnard also painted how rooms become invested with meaning over time and become "analogues of human experience," for they "contain memories and . . . stories" about our lives.

Bonnard's paintings of his home at Le Cannet show what it means to open yourself to the experience a particular place provides and how a new place can change an artist's artistic vision and the significance of the mundane events in your life. At Le Cannet, Bonnard challenged himself to record his home, not superficially, not as it appears to the eye, but instead as it developed meaning for him through the years and as it was transformed by time and memory. Bonnard's work at Le Cannet shows how the homes we move to can become mythic spaces if we pay them significant attention.

In his paintings, Bonnard depicted the freshness of the way we see a room for the first time, investing it with hope and possibility as we imagine the life we will live there. But he depicted, too, how we look at a room when we know it well, the wise sight that comes only with continued attention, familiarity, and love engendered by having spent much time there. In his paintings of the house at Le Cannet, some of which took twenty years to complete, Bonnard rendered how the eye sees a particular place at two different vantage points in time and how the mind remembers what it has seen even in seeing it anew.

Bonnard chose to spend much time deepening his relationship with very few things—the rooms of his home, the views from its windows, the attitude of Marthe in her bath—rather than flitting from subject to subject. Bonnard's profound relationship to his home grew because he was willing to pay attention to it, to study it, to paint it, day after day, year after year. Through this patient process he discovered "the lasting element in this fleetingness." "Emotion," he is recorded as saying, "comes in its own time." And freedom too: the freedom that results from the contemplation of everyday life, even sorrowful everyday life. And this contemplation requires that we provide ourselves with sufficient solitude and silence to undertake this soulful task.

For me, despite the riot of colors, the supersaturated yellows, apple greens, violets, and rusts, despite the outward appearance of domestic bliss, there is always an underlying pathos, even tragedy, in his work. The paintings seem to say that no matter how hard we try to create spaces where we will be happy, sorrow will nevertheless find us. And it is perhaps this awareness that deepens our connection to where we live.

You can see this, especially, in *La Fenêtre-ouverte* of 1921. At first, you see the open window, the shape of the mountain beyond, the green, green trees, the dark shade drawn somewhat down, the orange walls tinged with green, and tell yourself, "This is the room I want to live in." But then you notice Marthe slouched in a chair, looking not at the view, not at the simple astonishing beauty of this room, not at the flowers in the little cream vase with its blue shadows, but at a kitten who seems to look at her. Marthe reaches out her hand but she does not touch it; she is suspended in the moment between reaching and touching, emblematic of her relationship with the world. Her face is inscrutable, all enigma. Is this a rare moment of happiness in her grief-stricken days, as she tries to connect with a living being? Is this Marthe so sad that she cannot lift up her head, cannot quite touch the kitten? Or is this—and I have come to see the painting this way—a rare moment's joy passing over Marthe's features and leaving even as it has arrived. There can be no other reason for Bonnard to have painted her face in the way he has—more like the way a child would paint a face than an artist accomplished in emotional self-portraiture. No, I think Bonnard has painted what he wishes Marthe could have experienced but what she could not. The painting stands as testament to the fact that we might only experience transcendent joy in precious nanoseconds of time in a well-loved home.

We know from his biographers that Bonnard moved from working on one painting to another to another throughout the day, and through the years, reworked them again and again. Because he worked on them through time, returning to the paintings year after year, each became a record, not only of a moment frozen, a mood captured, but also of the shifts and changes in his perception.

After Marthe's death in 1942, Bonnard locked the door to her bedroom, left it as it was, and never entered it again. After Marthe's death, he continued revisiting paintings of her—a bath scene begun in 1941, paintings of the rooms in Le Cannet in which she became a "ghostly presence" lurking in the corners of his canvases. He painted portraits of himself as a man in deep mourning for Marthe, oblivious now, as never before, to his surroundings.

Bonnard died at Le Cannet in January 1947, leaving a treasure trove of paintings depicting how complex our relationship with a chosen home can become.

SIX

"Displaced"

Exiles, Refugees, Wanderers

THE LONELIEST PERSON WHO EVER LIVED . . .
No matter where she lived, throughout much of her life the poet Elizabeth Bishop felt homeless, like a "chronically displaced person," unable to experience the comfort and security of home. She attributed this to the tragic events of her childhood: her father's early death, her mother's madness and incarceration, her forced removal from the home of her beloved maternal grandparents by her paternal grandparents, who mistreated and neglected her. Bishop became the preeminent poet of recording humankind's desire for that special place called home where one can live a satisfying life. But she wrote, too, about how many of us are driven to pull up stakes and move on even after we've worked hard to make a home and about how fragmented we might feel if we are compelled to move continually, as Bishop did, hoping each new place will feel more like home.

Bishop's poetry describes how rare and blessed it is to feel truly at home and how painful it is not to feel at home where we live. Because Bishop herself felt at home so rarely, she could plumb the meaning of isolation. As she told a friend, "When you write my epitaph, you must say I was the loneliest person who ever lived."

In "The Sea and Its Shore," Bishop created a character who felt unable to feel at home anywhere, so he didn't live in a house but an "idea of a house." She wrote about the difference between inhabiting a house and merely living there: the first involves connecting to a home, merging with our surroundings, living differently from how we've lived in other places, and risking loving a place so much its loss will cause pain; the second involves holding back from a connection to a place, remaining immune to its charms, not forging a life specific to the home, staying fixed in our ways. Not allowing ourselves to love a house, Bishop believed, is rooted in some primal childhood terror and/or tragic moving experience early in life. Sadly, those who would profit most from forming a profound connection to a home might be unable to do so.

Elizabeth Bishop was born in 1911 in Worcester, Massachusetts. Her father died when she was eight months old. Throughout Bishop's childhood, her mother, Gertrude, was severely depressed, causing her to ignore and mistreat her daughter. Gertrude became so ill the family had no choice but to incarcerate her in a sanatorium, and no explanation was given to the young Elizabeth.

Before Gertrude was incarcerated, she and Elizabeth moved between Massachusetts and Gertrude's family home in Great Village, Nova Scotia, spending a few months at a time there; sometimes Elizabeth went alone. This place became Bishop's first real home, the one she often wrote about and dreamed about no matter where she lived. She lived there in 1916 and 1917 for about eighteen months, and visited summers when she attended boarding school. The look of Great Village—its blue sky, its brooks, its summer greens "with thick grass, elm trees, and evergreens running down to the rocky shore"—penetrated her senses.

The way of life in Great Village—simple, neighborly, hospitable—helped ease Bishop's loneliness. And she was made to feel at home in her grandparents' home—its parlor decorated with Indian artifacts, relatives' oil paintings, carpets and hooked rugs, a wallpaper of red-gray roses set against golden trellises. It felt like her own home. This house and village and the ways of those living there became touchstones against which Bishop compared the houses and neighborhoods of her adulthood and their mores, which she almost always found wanting—unless there was a significant similarity.

Throughout her life, Bishop often dreamed of buying a house near her grandparents' home. "I now see . . . a house in Nova Scotia on the bay," she wrote, "exactly like my grandmother's . . . Perhaps it is a recurrent need." At difficult times in her life, Bishop became nostalgic for the north, though she never moved back—perhaps because her life there was often difficult.

The peace of her grandparents' home was seriously compromised because of her mother's illness. "A scream, the echo of a scream, hangs over that Nova Scotian Village," Bishop wrote in an autobiographical work recounting her childhood mistreatment and abandonment: "First, she had come home, with her child. Then she had gone away again, alone, and left the child." Bishop was terrified by her mother's unpredictability and violence and felt unsafe when with her. Early, the idea of home became linked with terror. In that house, she wrote, many things were "damaged and lost, sickened or destroyed." After her mother's permanent incarceration, Bishop never saw her again. After seventeen years in the sanatorium, her mother died there in 1934, when Bishop was in her twenties.

Through the years, Bishop lived with her father's family and other relatives. In a late, unfinished poem, Bishop examined the trauma of those incessant early moves: "Change is what hurts worst; change alone can kill."

In young adulthood, when visiting friends and relatives made Bishop acutely feel the pain of her homelessness, she developed a passion for travel. As she described in *Questions of Travel*, a voyager is not supposed to feel at home. When visiting a new place, her feelings of homelessness abated and she temporarily felt at ease: "I guess I have liked to travel as much as I have," she wrote, "because I have always felt isolated."

Bishop preferred foreign travel, especially to out-of-the-way places: Newfoundland; Douarnenez, France; Morocco; Majorca; Haiti; the Amazon (about which she wrote "On the Amazon" and "Santarém"); the Galápagos; Ecuador; Peru; Stockholm; Helsinki; Leningrad; Bergen, Norway; Rotterdam, the Netherlands; Portugal; the Greek Islands. Before traveling to a new destination, she would read about it and make lists of sights she wanted to visit. In a letter to a friend, she quoted W. H. Auden's saying: " 'Geography is a thousand times more important to modern man than history.' " And, she added, "I always like to *feel* exactly where I am geographically all the time, on the map."

Back in the States after her first trip abroad in 1935, to France, England, Morocco, and Spain, Bishop traveled to Florida, falling into an ambivalent love with the state—"The state with the prettiest name, / the state that floats in brackish water." With Louise Crane, she bought a house in Key West in 1938. It stood in a garden with banana, avocado, lime, mango, and soursop trees. This was the first house she loved. Later, she shared the house with

Marjorie Carr Stevens. Her letters from Key West were often geography lessons—Bishop was keenly aware of *place*, of geography: vegetation, climate, birds, and insects; landscape, rivers, and seascapes. She learned what grew well and began a garden with "a lettuce bed, radishes, carrots, mint, parsley."

In Key West, Bishop discovered she preferred to decorate her homes provisionally, wanting them to feel like encampments. She adorned the Key West home with found objects and art and artifacts by locals. Her home there resembled a small museum.

She discovered new pleasures like swimming, fishing, boating, and gardening, all of which enriched her life, for they enabled her to see her body in a new way: not as a site of disease—she had debilitating allergies and asthma—but as one of power and pleasure. These new pursuits, her new landscape, and her Key West home became subjects for her work. But not subjects in the traditional sense. For Bishop developed a poetics dedicated to examining *a mind thinking* about what she saw, experienced, and felt. She worked hard at rendering the process of living a life in a specific place and how that process was often encumbered by a painful past.

Key West was "a fresh start" for her, a phrase she often used when she moved, hoping that moving could erase her pain, change her life. In every new place, she hoped she'd be free from the demons haunting her—alcoholism, allergies and asthma, difficulty working, feelings of homelessness. Though moving never did precipitate a complete life change, there were blessed spaces of time when this seemed possible—in Key West and later in Brazil.

Moving always afforded a fresh start for Bishop's work, however, for it forced her into an intimate and profound connection with place—her senses became sharp, and her poems capture the immediacy of her early impressions. She began some of her most important poems when she was new to a place.

Bishop loved to live in "temporary homes by the sea." They brought back the ease she'd sometimes felt in Nova Scotia. She liked the simplification, improvisation, and community these places could provide. "You live in this Robinson Crusoe atmosphere," she wrote, ". . . contriving and inventing." She'd live in and visit many such places throughout her life—North Haven, Maine; West Falmouth and Cuttyhunk, Massachusetts. Bishop celebrated this kind of life in her masterwork "Crusoe in England."

When visiting seaside places, Bishop wrote more. She seemed more content as a visitor in someone else's home or when she was traveling than she did in her own home: "I've rarely written anything of value at the desk or in the room where I was supposed to be doing it," she wrote, "—it's always in someone else's house." Sometimes, though, dislocation inhibited her.

Given Bishop's painful family history, staying with friends so she wouldn't be alone and traveling seemed more satisfying than living in one place. Even in her beloved Key West home, restlessness overcame her. Whether settled or traveling, though, she learned she could never be rid of a wrenching homesickness so profound it felt like "a deathly physical and mental *illness.*"

In her Key West journal, Bishop recorded her terror during her debilitating asthma attacks. She described how people with chronic illnesses often feel unsafe in their homes. During the worst of times, when she was never able to relax, never sure if she would survive the day, no place ever truly felt safe, truly felt like home.

When Bishop wrote about home, she often used metaphors for being closeted, caged, trapped, smothered, and suffocated. No wonder, then, that she wanted to leave wherever she lived, that she resided uneasily in each of her homes, that she wanted to move on to another place where she might find relief.

While in Brazil, Bishop wrote the poem "Arrival at Santos": "Here is a coast," she wrote, "here is a harbor / . . . Oh, tourist, / is this how this country is going to answer you / and your immodest demands for a different world, / and a better life . . . ?"

Bishop described her years in Brazil as the happiest of her life. Settling there came as a surprise. When she first arrived in November 1951, she had no plans to stay. The stop in Rio de Janeiro was a way station on a sea voyage circumnavigating South America. Bishop spent a few days visiting friends, including Lota de Macedo Soares, a member of a prominent Brazilian family and a self-trained architect whom Bishop had met in New York.

Lota took Bishop to visit Petrópolis, in the mountains some sixty miles from Rio. There, in a spectacular setting, Lota was building her ultramodern "transparent" house, Fazenda Samambaia, constructed mostly of glass. When completed, it would become known as the best modern house in Brazil.

Bishop had always loved architecture and was mesmerized by the nuts and bolts of how raw materials were turned into houses. Wherever she went, she studied domestic architecture and remarked on what she learned in her letters.

Bishop realized the grandeur of Lota's vision. Lota was building a house on a difficult, steep site, backing it against a black granite cliff next to a waterfall, incorporating "the rigidity of iron," "the fragility of glass," and "the roughness of rocks from the river" into the design. Lota told Bishop about her vision of constructing a private pool beside the waterfall encircled by native vegetation, a place to swim on sultry days.

Bishop was entranced with the construction of Fazenda Samambaia and fell in love with its gorgeous surroundings. This place was different from anything Bishop had experienced, "a sort of dream-combination of plant & animal life." She imagined living there, learning the names of the flowers and trees, imagined she could be happy there.

During Bishop's visit, Lota was kind, hospitable, and generous—even caring for Bishop when she developed a severe allergic reaction after eating a cashew. Lota invited Bishop to prolong her stay and to move into the under-construction Fazenda Samambaia, which was just barely habitable. Though Lota lived there with another woman, Lota's kindness and their growing feelings for each other, along with the chance to live in an architectural rarity in a stunning landscape near a series of historic sites, made Bishop decide to stay. Fazenda Samambaia seemed like the home Bishop had wished for all her life, her first "real home."

Soon, Bishop and Lota became lovers. Bishop thought their love was a classic case of "opposites attract." Lota was "manorial, powerful, quick"; Bishop, "hesitant, full of vagaries." Still, they shared much: both had lost their parents early in life, and it had profoundly affected both of them. Lota supported Bishop so she could write poetry without worrying about finances. With Lota's help, Bishop got her drinking under control for a time. Life on the estate replicated what Bishop had yearned for—a sense of community that came from Lota's nearby family, an improvisational life of "making do" in a place that was more construction site than home.

In Brazil, Bishop shifted her sense of time. She felt free of a chronic awareness of the passage of time while she was there. "Time is [now]," she wrote, "nothing if not amenable."

Bishop and Lota established a routine—what Bishop called "rites of conviviality." They ate breakfast in bed; inspected the work site; made their menu and grocery list; ate lunch; opened and responded to mail; ate supper; conversed and read—often aloud to each other. They made plans: they would raise cows and churn their own butter; they would travel; Bishop would plant a garden with brussels sprouts, artichokes, corn, watercress, mint, lilies, agapanthus, azaleas, alyssum, phlox, sweet william, and iris. Many of these plans materialized, though Lota did not like traveling, and her intense work on the beautification of Flamengo Park in Rio kept her from leaving Brazil.

Bishop embraced the domestic life. She cooked; made jam from local fruits like the jaboticaba; baked fruitcakes and plum puddings at Christmas and baked healthy breads—oatmeal, raisin, and wheat germ—in a specially built outdoor wood-burning oven. Lota called her "Cookie."

Lota built a writing studio for Bishop, a private retreat with a workspace, kitchenette, and bathroom set in a clump of bamboo overlooking a creek and the waterfall. As she worked, Bishop could hear the sound of running water. Bishop decorated her studio with Chinese art objects in blue and white. For the first time in years, she could gather her collection of books and her manuscripts together in one place. She readied herself to write in a way that would be "a new departure."

For a time, Bishop was more productive than ever before. She worked without her typical crippling anxiety, creating poems and sketches based on her childhood: "Gwendolyn," "In the Village," "Memories of Uncle Neddy," "The Country Mouse," "The Moose." It seemed the serenity of her Brazilian life allowed her to examine and write about her difficult childhood. But much of her work was based on her new life: "Squatter's Children," "Manuelzinho," "Questions of Travel," "A Trip to Vigia," "Electrical Storm," and translations and compilations of Brazilian works including

The Diary of Helena Morley (Minha Vida de Menina) and *Black Beans and Diamonds*, an anthology of Brazilian poetry Bishop coedited. She felt a newfound pride in her work, especially after winning the Pulitzer Prize in 1956.

Her happiness in Brazil was due, in great measure, to her love for Lota, to their sharing a home, for she believed "happiness does not consist in worldly goods but in a peaceful home, in family affection." And she loved Brazil too. "I like it so much," she wrote, "that I keep thinking I have died and gone to heaven, completely undeservedly." All seemed to go well if Bishop kept her drinking under control.

But in time, Bishop began to "drink herself unconscious," although Lota tried to keep her on Antabuse. She began to feel estranged from Lota, resenting Lota's work and her financial dependence on her. She began to feel trapped and isolated at Samambaia when Lota wasn't there; she wanted to travel.

When life with Lota became too painful, Bishop returned to the United States for a cooling-off period in their relationship, hoping that Lota would later join her. But living with Bishop had become too difficult for Lota. There were a few failed attempts at reconciliation in Brazil. Finally, on a trip to New York to meet Bishop, Lota took an overdose of tranquilizers and died after being in a coma for five days. She and Bishop had been together fourteen years.

Thereafter, Bishop moved to and from Brazil several times, trying to establish a life for herself in a home she'd bought at Ouro Preto that she wanted to restore to its original glory. She taught writing at prestigious universities, entered and left treatment centers for alcoholism, established relationships with other women, visited friends in seaside houses.

During her last years, Bishop settled in an apartment on

Boston's Lewis Wharf with a view of the harbor and the Old North Church. She furnished it with belongings brought from Brazil—a Venetian mirror, a jacaranda rocking chair, a Franklin stove, a carved figurehead, her enormous library.

But wherever she lived, she was conscious of her lost homes in Brazil: the house she'd shared with Lota, the house in Ouro Preto she'd never managed to fix up. In an early draft of her villanelle "One Art," she chronicled all her losses, the "losses nobody can master": the loss of a lover; of the places she loved— "one peninsula and one island," "a small-sized town," "a splendid beach," "a good-sized bay," "a good piece of one continent," "another continent."

In "The End of March," she described, "my proto-dream-house, / my crypto-dream-house." It was a house she'd seen by the sea where she imagined she might live an idyllic life she understood she could never realize. It was a "crooked box / set up on pilings, shingld green, . . . / . . . I'd like to retire there and do *nothing*, / or nothing much, forever, in two bare rooms: / look through binoculars, read boring books, / . . . write down useless notes, / talk to myself . . . / A light to read by—perfect! But impossible."

At the end of her life, Bishop realized she was wrong in believing she had moved about during her life to find a better place to live. What she'd really always wanted, she concluded, was a perfect partnership like the one she'd shared with Lota.

LIBERATION MINGLED WITH MOURNING . . .
On March 12, 1938, Sigmund Freud sat by his radio in his home at Berggasse 19 in Vienna "listening to the sound of Germans taking over Austria." Soon the streets of Vienna were filled with tanks and people shouting "Heil Hitler." In his March 13 diary

entry, Freud wrote, "Anschluss with Germany"; on March 14, "Hitler in Vienna."

Jews in Austria immediately began to suffer greater outrages than any ever previously committed elsewhere under the Third Reich. Catholic prelates celebrated Hitler's conquest in churches; Jews were beaten; Jewish merchants were boycotted; property owned by Jews was stolen, damaged, or destroyed; Jewish professionals were purged. The German playwright Carl Zuckmayer, eyewitness to these events, reported that overnight Vienna was "transformed into a nightmare painting by Hieronymus Bosch." According to Peter Gay, Freud's biographer, "The . . . sadistic vengefulness it had taken many Germans five years . . . to express, Austrians learned to act out in as many days." Five hundred Jews committed suicide rather than face the inevitable—continuing persecution, deportation to concentration camps. Even Freud's daughter, Anna, asked her father whether they should kill themselves, to which Freud replied, "Why? Because they would like us to?"

Since Hitler's invasion, the Gestapo had Freud "under constant surveillance." The Aryan owner of Freud's house had painted a swastika over his door. Heinrich Himmler wanted to put Freud's "gang of analysts" in prison immediately but was restrained. Still, Freud was reluctant to depart because he believed he was too old and infirm to travel and that no country would offer him asylum; even after his home was invaded and searched for anti-Nazi documents twice and his son Martin was arrested and held prisoner all day, Freud wanted to remain.

In time Freud began to understand his situation was dire, though he believed he couldn't escape the country because his passport had been confiscated. "I am waiting," he wrote his friend Arnold Zweig, "with ever increasing regret, for the curtain to fall for me." Still, he thought emigrating "would be like a soldier deserting his post." In rebuttal, Ernest Jones told Freud that though the second officer of the *Titanic* did not want to leave his ship, nonetheless, his ship left him. Jones's words, together with Anna Freud's capture (she was released, though for a time she thought she would remain a prisoner and no doubt be executed), helped persuade Freud to leave, and he began to wish he could "die in freedom."

Freud moved to London, where his son Ernst lived, after three months of negotiations at the highest levels of government in the United States and elsewhere to secure his release. The move was made with more than two thousand pieces of Freud's precious collection of art objects and archaeological artifacts and his large library of archaeology texts. Still, much of his library, many of his possessions, and all his ready money and savings were confiscated. Before leaving, Freud burned many of his papers and much of his correspondence.

Before the move of his artifacts was assured, when he feared he would lose his entire collection, Freud selected two representative pieces, a statue of the goddess Athena and a Qing Dynasty jade screen, to smuggle out of Austria. With them safe, as talismans, he believed he could survive the move and carry on his life in a new place. Through the years, the collection had become extremely important to Freud; he felt the objects were an extension of himself and moving them was necessary for his well-being.

While waiting for final arrangements, Freud's household showed few signs of the family's imminent departure. Routine, at this juncture, seemed essential. Freud continued to work on his book about Moses and a translation of a work by Samuel Butler. He began speaking of himself as "Ahasverus," the wandering Jew who would come to rest somewhere. Viewing his coming exile in the larger context of the history of the Jews seemed to give him hope. That he would most likely "die in freedom" cheered him.

Before his exodus, Freud was made to sign a document stating he'd been well treated by the Nazis. He added the sentence "I can most highly recommend the Gestapo to everyone"—a dangerous defiant gesture that went unnoticed.

Freud finally left Vienna on June 4, 1938, accompanied by his wife, his daughter, and a physician. Other members of his party—selected students and their families—left at other times. Freud was eighty-three. A "triumphant feeling of liberation," he wrote when he arrived in London, "is mingled too strongly with mourning, for one had still very much loved the prison from which one has been released."

Freud's beloved collection also arrived safely in London. After the family was settled in 20 Maresfield Gardens in Hampstead Heath, Freud's architect son, Ernst, renovated his father's study to "reproduce, as closely as possible" his Vienna office, and Freud's maid Paula Fichtl arranged his collection precisely as it had been, assisted by photographs taken by Edmund Engelman. The presence of his beloved collection somewhat eased the trauma of exile and relocation.

Even before Freud left Austria, his daughter, Anna, remarked, "Moving with us is always a lengthy and strenuous business." Freud never felt at home unless he had his immense collection with him, and whenever the family traveled from their Vienna home to summer in the mountains near Berchtesgaden, his wife, Martha, and Paula Fichtl packed and moved many of his artifacts, his "old and grubby gods." These statues took part in his work, Freud said. They functioned as "paperweights for my manuscripts." But the poet H. D., an analysand of Freud, believed these objects reminded Freud of the past and the locus of his discovery—that "the childhood of the individual is the childhood of the race." H. D. believed the statues posed questions: they "stare and stare and seem to say, what has happened to you?" she wrote. According to Janine Burke, an expert on the collection, Freud became obsessed with beautiful ancient mythic objects. In time, he acquired a "private museum of more than 2000 statues, vases, . . . fragments of papyrus, rings, precious stones and prints." He collected "neolithic tools, delicate Sumerian seals . . . , Egyptian mummy bandages . . . , superb Hellenistic statues, images of the sphinx, erotic Roman charms, . . . and Chinese jade lions." He possessed many statues of Eros, one, a Greek terra-cotta, better than those in the Louvre; another of Eros as a child. There were also many representations of female deities, "Isis, Athena, Artemis and Venus." These surrounded him as he worked; one, a statue of "Isis Suckling the Infant Horus, an Egyptian bronze from around 664BC," was displayed on his desk.

Freud began his collection in 1896 after his father's death and while he was writing *The Interpretation of Dreams*. Freud's first acquisition was a set of Florentine plaster casts. Once he started collecting, he didn't stop. Collecting shifted his self-image: he became "a conquistador, an adventurer, . . . with all the inquisitiveness, daring and tenacity capable of such a man."

He tried to understand his sudden obsessive desire to acquire ancient artifacts, concluding, "In my inner self, I now feel quite uprooted." Collecting, then, became an antidote to his feeling psychically unsettled, a profound insight on Freud's part, for he came to understand how significant people's special possessions are in giving them a sense of psychic wholeness, how the presence of these possessions can ease trying times and difficult transitions, and how their loss can be traumatic, perhaps even catastrophic.

Some biographers have interpreted Freud's acquiring disinterred objects as a symbolic attempt to bring his father back to life, and perhaps on one level it was. Others believe the collection signified Freud's preoccupation with death and perhaps represented his awareness of life's fleetingness. Whatever his inner motive, these objects memorialized "loss and absence, grief and memory, elegy and mourning." But they also honored the artistic impulse and one man's knowledge of how wisely acquired beautiful objects can salve the human spirit during times of change.

H. D. believed Freud regarded his objects as family members, connecting him to the history of the human race, for they reached "back through . . . the Roman Empire, further into the Holy Land." "He is part and parcel of these treasures," H. D. said. Ernest Jones described how when Freud acquired something special, he brought it to the dinner table and placed it "in front of him as a companion." His favorite piece was a broken bronze statuette of the goddess Athena missing her spear. Without his collection, Freud believed a precious part of himself would be lost.

In his Vienna study, surrounded by his gods, Freud contemplated the workings of his own psyche and speculated on how to codify and describe the commonality of human experience. They came to represent those mythic archetypes of human history he used to unlock the mystery of his own personal history and those of his patients, so many of whom exhibited problems dealing with and healing from a sense of emptiness and dislocation. Freud's collection thus played a significant role in his autoanalysis, in his theoretical work, and in his treatment of patients.

In time these objects came to represent Freud's intellectual and emotional journey in trying to explain why people behaved as they did. As art objects, they represented the deepest, most ineffable desires of humankind. They kept him company during those long hours of solitude when, after his father's death, he began his autoanalysis, "plunging into his own unconscious, the underground recesses of his buried self." Because they accompanied this difficult journey, he became extremely attached to them: "I must always have an object to love," he told Carl Jung. His collection provided "a feeling of sacred peace and quiet," according to his patient Sergei Pankejeff, known as the Wolf Man. Pankejeff remarked that in entering Freud's study, one felt one was "leaving the haste of modern life behind, of being sheltered from one's daily cares."

Freud had pondered how to make a comfortable home even before he married. Writing to Martha while the two were courting, he described his ideal home: "Two or three little rooms. . . . Tables and chairs, beds, mirrors, a clock to remind the happy couple of the passage of time, an armchair for an hour's pleasant daydreaming, carpets to help the housewife keep the floors clean, linen tied with pretty ribbons in the cupboard . . . , pictures on the walls, glasses for everyday and others for wine and festive occasions. . . . And there will be so much to enjoy, the books and the sewing table and the cosy lamp."

Before the wedding, Freud himself furnished the apartment, aiming for "solid Victorian comfort." He bought "embroidered tablecloths, plush-covered chairs, . . . a profusion of oriental rugs." The family kept the furnishings throughout his life in Vienna. Home was the site of pleasure, and Freud believed everything that could be done should be done to make it pleasurable.

Years before he became a collector, Freud visited the home of his mentor Jean-Martin Charcot in Paris and saw how Charcot had appointed his study with antiquities—Gobelin tapestries, Indian and Chinese antiques. Charcot inspired Freud to study neurosis. But he also influenced Freud's vision of what constituted a "distinctive home and work environment" that would be a source of pleasure and inspiration.

On January 28, 1939, Virginia and Leonard Woolf went to visit Sigmund Freud at his London home and took tea with him in his library. The Woolfs had been publishing Freud's works since 1924, when the Hogarth Press obtained the rights to a complete authorized English translation of Freud's collected papers. Leonard Woolf said that "the greatest pleasure" he got from publishing Freud was their relationship, remarking that Freud was not only a genius, "but . . . an extraordinarily nice man." Publishing these papers was a bold venture for a fledgling press, but it was extremely successful. Subsequently, the Hogarth Press published an English translation of every book Freud wrote, and after his death, it would bring out a standard edition of his complete works.

This visit was the first and only time the Woolfs met Freud, and both wrote an account—Virginia in her diary, Leonard in his autobiography. Freud was suffering from cancer—it had first been detected in 1923 in his jaw and palate—and he was but eight months away from death. He didn't look well. Virginia described him as "a screwed up shrunk very old man: with monkeys light eyes, paralysed spasmodic movements, inarticulate: but alert"; Leonard said Freud projected an air of "great gentleness," but behind it "great strength." Leonard remarked that he was "extraordinarily courteous" throughout the meeting, though he was like "a half-extinct volcano" with "something sombre, suppressed, reserved" in his nature. Though many famous people are either "disappointing or bores, or both," Leonard said he thought Freud instead "had an aura, not of fame, but of greatness." When they discussed Freud's notoriety, Freud remarked that he was "infamous rather than famous."

Conversation was difficult, because of both Freud's illness and the language barrier, and Freud's daughter helped interpret. Freud spoke about the impact of Hitler, about how he believed it would take a generation "before the poison will be worked out." Virginia remarked she and Leonard "felt some guilt" for what had happened to the Jews, for if England had not won the war in 1914, there would have been "no Nazis and no Hitler." Freud told her he believed it would have been worse had Germany won the war, that Hitler and the Nazis would have gained power in any event.

What impressed Leonard most was that Freud's study was "very light, shining, clean, with a pleasant, open view through the windows into a garden" and filled with an abundance of antiquities. During the visit, Freud gave Woolf a narcissus. What impressed Virginia most was Freud's immense collection of artifacts: "Sitting in a great library with little statues at a large scrupulously tidy shiny table," Woolf wrote. "We like patients on chairs."

Soon after this meeting, Virginia first began reading Freud's work. At the time, Woolf was reviewing her life, writing a memoir, and contemplating the meaning of the sexual abuse she'd experienced in childhood and its effect on her psyche. She believed it was responsible for her neurosis. But reading Freud's seduction theory perhaps caused her to suspect that she'd imagined those experiences or that she herself invited them. This shift in her perspective might have contributed to the depression preceding her suicide.

Freud chose to die not in his bedroom but in the study where Virginia and Leonard Woolf had met him, in the place where he wrote and practiced psychoanalysis, surrounded by the "pagan splendour" of his collection. During his last days, he gazed out the window into the garden. He entered a coma and died after his doctor administered the fatal dose of morphine he requested, ending his sixteen-year battle with cancer.

H. D. later wrote she was happy Freud died "before the blast and bombing and fires . . . devastated this city" where he and his family had taken refuge. Before he died, Freud, suspecting London would be attacked and that many would die, expressed concern for the fate of his grandchildren.

FOREVER ON THE MOVE . . .

Even at the end of his life, when he was seriously ill with tuberculosis, so ill that he spent most of his time in bed, D. H. Lawrence was one of the most peripatetic writers who ever lived. From 1927—when Lawrence experienced the first of a series of serious hemorrhages—through 1930, Lawrence and his wife, Frieda, lived in a series of inns, hotels, borrowed houses, and rented villas; they also visited friends and family for extended periods. During this time, though much weakened, Lawrence composed *Lady Chatterley's Lover*, one of his masterworks.

In these last years, with little energy to spare from the difficult work of simply staying alive and writing—they needed his income and were often nearly destitute—Lawrence and Frieda lived in the Villa Mirenda at San Polo a Mosciano, southwest of Florence; with the Huxleys in Forte dei Marmi in Tuscany; with Frieda's sister Johanna at Villach in Austria to see if it helped Lawrence breathe more easily (it did, for a time). They moved into a borrowed house in Irschenhausen in Bavaria; moved back to the Villa Mirenda; considered moving back to Eastwood, in the English Midlands, where Lawrence lived as a child, but didn't;

joined their friends the Huxleys at Les Diablerets in Switzerland; considered moving back to their ranch in New Mexico but didn't; moved to the Grand Hotel in Chexbres-sur-Vevey, on the north side of Lake Geneva in Switzerland, to escape the summer's heat in Italy; lived in a rented chalet, the Chalet Kesselmatte, in Gsteig in Switzerland for a summer; visited Frieda's mother in Baden-Baden, where the Lawrences decided to give up the Villa Mirenda; moved to Le Lavandou near Toulon; lived with friends for the winter in La Vigie on the island of Port Cros, where Lawrence became increasingly ill, so they decided to move on; journeyed by boat to Toulon and then along the coast for a few weeks; settled in the Hotel Beau-Rivage in Bandol, where Lawrence felt at home for the first time in a long while; journeyed to Paris to see to the private publication of *Lady Chatterley's Lover*; moved to Majorca; returned to visit the Huxleys in Forte dei Marmi; lived in his publisher's flat in Florence; moved into the Hotel Lowen in Baden-Baden; visited Kurhaus Plätig in the Black Forest, where his condition worsened; moved to Rottach-am-Tegernsee in the Bavarian Alps, where Lawrence came to believe the altitude was wrong for him (here, they had virtually no furnishings, but they had a potted gentian bush, about which Lawrence wrote the poem "Bavarian Gentians"); moved back to the Beau-Rivage in Bandol, where Lawrence believed he was able to breathe more easily; moved into the bungalow Villa Beau Soleil in Bandol, right on the sea, with wonderful air and light; moved into the sanatorium Ad Astra in the mountains of Vence (for this move, Lawrence packed his own trunk and tidied the villa for Frieda before leaving); moved into the Villa Robermond in Vence because he believed the sanatorium wasn't doing him any good and because he didn't want to die there; dreamed of returning to their ranch in New Mexico but couldn't, because now

Lawrence was near death. He died in the Villa Robermond in Vence.

All told, Lawrence moved about a hundred times during his last seventeen years; he was only in his mid-forties when he died and didn't begin to move often until he was in his late twenties. He moved, on average, five to six times a year, when others as sick as he was would have stayed put. Of all the writers whose lives I've studied, Lawrence takes the prize for moving most often.

The question is, *Why?* What makes a person lead such an unsettled life?

The story begins with D. H. Lawrence's parents, who, before they settled in Eastwood, Nottinghamshire, moved often during the eight years of their marriage before Lawrence was born in 1885. As Lawrence has written, his mother, Lydia Lawrence, was at first attracted to Arthur, her charismatic, virile, miner husband. But after their marriage, she wanted a better life for herself and her children. His life as a collier was one of constant, backbreaking toil, and he came home at night blackened from the pits, famished from his day's work, wanting his meal before he took a wash. She fancied herself better than him: she'd been a teacher, read philosophy, wrote poetry. His filthy presence at the table, crude manners, and drinking disgusted her. She did not want her husband to claim her son David Herbert for the pit, and she turned him against his father.

Because he was sickly, Lydia coddled her son, kept him with her as a companion, and he became something of a monster. He acted as if the world should be organized to satisfy him and refused to change his ways to suit what others expected of him. This would turn out to be one of the causes of his constant moving: nowhere was ever good enough for him; the next place might be better.

Lawrence's mother did not keep her dissatisfaction from her son. She was "scornful," according to Lawrence, of where they lived and Lawrence continually heard his mother's grievances against her living situation and husband. She hated their house in the Breach, the community built for miners. She hated the view of ash pits from the back of the house. She hated the noise, the smoke, the clanking headstock. She believed she was made for a better life.

When Lawrence was six, the family moved to another house in the Breach, but with a wonderful view. After a short time, they moved again. Each time, Lydia hoped the new place would better suit her. But soon enough she became dissatisfied and wanted to move on—a pattern Lawrence would repeat throughout his adult life. Lydia told her son he could realize her dreams for him only by leaving Eastwood. Early, Lawrence learned that the meaning of home was dissatisfaction and disaffection; home was not a place to stay but rather a place to leave. Still, as a grown man, much as he criticized the Midlands, he often idealized it, referring to the area as "the country of my heart."

Lydia always wanted there be something different, something special distinguishing her home from those of the other colliers' families—a nicer view, a bigger window, a corner lot, a bit of garden. Still, she was never satisfied, hoping always that if she found the right place, a "proper" home, it would change her life, a belief she passed on to her son. She instilled in him a chronic yearning for an unattainable ideal that propelled Lawrence, as an adult, from one place to another, sometimes after a few months, sometimes after a few weeks, but sometimes, too, after a few days. Each time he moved, Lawrence hoped the next place would match his ideals, but it rarely did.

During Lawrence's boyhood, there was much hostility and

open warfare between his parents, both because of his mother's unhappiness and his father's drinking. Lawrence told a friend that his household resembled "Hades." Near their home was a brook, hedgerows, and open land into which Lawrence escaped often. There, he first developed a passion for nature and first understood how his troubled spirit could be healed by it. Lawrence's love of the countryside was engendered, too, by his childhood friendship with Jessie Chambers and her family; throughout his life, he recalled his visits to the Chambers family farm, Haggs, as a "golden time": it was one of the very few places where Lawrence felt "absolutely at home," and it seems as if he searched—and failed to find—another place where he would feel so happy.

Lydia instilled a restless spirit in Lawrence, but she also taught him high standards for where a home should be and what it should look like. She worked hard at decorating her houses, and, this, too, Lawrence learned—to beautify wherever he lived, no matter how humble his circumstances.

After Lawrence met Frieda Weekley in 1912 and she left her husband and children to be with him and later marry him, the couple moved constantly in search of the ideal place to settle. He wanted to live in a foreign place to satisfy his sense of adventure and excitement. He wanted his home to be beautifully situated in a country setting, unmarred by any evidence of industry, preferably high on a hill. He wanted a grand view, preferably of a body of water—near the sea, Lawrence felt more in touch with "the clean world," unpolluted by the presence of human beings; he loved the sea's constant motion, its strength and power, and he became calm near it. He wanted to live in a place where people lived "authentic" lives—Lawrence's peregrination through Sardinia in 1921 was undertaken because he wanted to find a place where an "indomitable" maleness still existed. He needed air that he could easily breathe—Lawrence thought that if only he could find the "right location and the right attitude to life," he would recover from his tuberculosis. He wanted to be in a remote location where he and Frieda wouldn't be bombarded with guests, allowing him to write without interruption; even though, when isolated, the couple fought. And paradoxically, he wanted to be near a community of like-minded people with whom he could socialize, but only when he chose to.

Surprisingly, Lawrence very often found such places, even though the quarters he and Frieda inhabited might be borrowed, modest, or even derelict. A farmhouse in Gargnano on Lake Garda in Italy. A cottage in Fiascherino on the Bay of Spezia. A cottage near Chesham in Buckinghamshire. A rustic abode in Porthcorthan in Cornwall. A place in Picinisco in the wilds of Abruzzi. A villa in Taormina in Sicily. A bungalow in New South Wales, Australia. A ranch outside Taos, New Mexico (the home he most longed to return to as he was dying). A house in Chapala, Mexico.

Lawrence hoped to find a place—perhaps in Florida—where he could establish a utopian community, one isolated from the ills of the modern world. There, like-minded people would live communally "in a better way than conventional society permitted." He envisioned his friend Lady Ottoline Morrell as the keystone of this community—perhaps he thought she would fund it—which would be called Rananim. He solicited his friends for membership in such a community throughout his life. Often, Lawrence believed that living with Frieda wasn't satisfying enough for him; he wanted to live close to a man with whom he could establish a "blood brotherhood," which might, or might not, include sex. Still, the Lawrences' single attempt at communal living, with Katherine Mansfield and John Middleton Murry in Cornwall, was a dismal failure. Yet when he was isolated, he could become depressed because he felt like an outsider: "I do not belong . . . at all, at all." During his life, Lawrence felt truly at home in only four places: Zennor, on the coast of Cornwall; Fontana Vecchia in Taormina, Sicily; the Villa Mirenda, "looking far out over the the Val d'Arno" in Tuscany; and the Del Monte Ranch in Questa, New Mexico.

Even if his quarters were temporary, when able, Lawrence worked hard to make them more livable, to turn the place into his "own home." He scrubbed grime off brick floors, put up shelves, made a dresser or a cabinet, painted the walls (in Zennor, they were pale pink), decorated pots and jars, borrowed furnishings or bought them at flea markets, sewed curtains, adorned the place with flowers. If he lived in a place long enough, he gardened, planting vegetables and flowers; in Zennor, he made three gardens, one of which provided excellent meals for their table.

Lawrence was a househusband who cooked, cleaned, and decorated. He was almost completely responsible for running the household, which included making travel plans, arranging for moves, communicating with the outside world. All this, while he was earning their keep, often writing well over two thousand words a day. Frieda believed her mission in life was to be a *Magner Mater*, the strength behind Lawrence's genius. Having grown up with servants, she did relatively little, if anything, in the way of housework—Lawrence even had to teach her to fold her clothing and keep it neat. A few times she house hunted for them, but not often. Even when Lawrence was ill, he waited on her and she barely tended him.

As a child, Lawrence had become enraged if he couldn't control the way people acted, if they didn't act the way he expected them to. This trait continued into adulthood, but it extended, too, to the places he lived. Lawrence would become furious if the place where he moved didn't turn out to be what he'd expected. He continually sought a place that would fulfill his "nostalgia for something I know not what." He would read or hear about a place he believed might be suitable, imagine what it would be like living there, assume it would be better than where he was currently living, decide to relocate, break up house, and move on. Sometimes they would move great distances on nothing more than a whim—as when they moved to Australia from Ceylon; someone Lawrence met had described Australia to him and extended an invitation, and it sounded like a fascinating place to live.

Once in a new place, Lawrence would put it to the test. Sometimes it suited him and he stayed for a while. But as soon as he found something wrong, or he wasn't treated as he thought he should be by anyone he encountered, or if the local inhabitants weren't living as authentically as he thought they should be (and authenticity seemed to mean living a life unspoiled by modern civilization), or if something about the house stopped suiting him, or if he became ill while he was there, then he would become restless at best, or fly into a rage at worst, and feel the compulsion to move on. He would pack up, move to the next idealized place, and live there until it too stopped suiting him.

At times Lawrence understood the source of his chronic dissatisfaction. He remarked that people with a childhood like his were condemned to look for, but never find, the ideal place to live, a new Canaan. His character Birkin in *Women in Love* remarked he wanted "to wander away from the world's somewheres, into our own nowhere," paralleling Lawrence's view. When Lawrence decided to leave England in early 1912 after writing "Paul Morel" (which metamorphosed into *Sons and Lovers*), he viewed it as a "break from the past." When he moved to Germany in the spring of 1912 to meet Frieda before they married, he described it as an escape from England. When he moved to the United States, he said he wanted to "cut clear of the old world—burn one's boats."

He thought that a new place would mean a new life for him. When he moved to Irschenhausen, he felt "cut off from my past life—like a re-incarnation." Staring across the English Channel to Dover, he thought about "another kind of life that might be lived abroad." When he and Frieda moved to Gargnano, he said he went there to undertake the difficult project of changing himself. When he moved to Porthcothan in Cornwall, he said he would experience "a new life." When he and Frieda moved to Ceylon, he was eager to see more of the world and wanted "a new *start*"; by then he was sick of Europe and he moved even though he thought that Ceylon wouldn't suit him, that his stay would be impermanent, and that he would only "make more ends."

Two events made Lawrence leave England for good and precipitated his and Frieda's wanderings in foreign lands: the censorship of Lawrence's novel *The Rainbow* and their expulsion from Cornwall during World War I.

Lawrence believed *The Rainbow* was the finest expression of his art. But it was seized, banned, and burned as obscene and offensive to society; a directive was issued for all copies of the novel and the plates to be destroyed. "I curse them all . . . to eternal damnation," Lawrence wrote when he heard of the order. If he stayed in England, he believed he would die because the place was "poisonous." He said, too, that it "oppresses one's lungs, one cannot breathe." He wanted to "live apart from the foul world which I will not accept or acknowledge." But he did not move abroad until 1919.

During World War I, because Frieda was German, they were suspected of being spies, signaling German submarines off the Cornwall coast with flashlights, and were forced to leave their home in Zennor, a place Lawrence felt, for the first time, at home. The Lawrences lived in a cottage overlooking the water near a shipping lane, and during their residence, more than forty-nine ships were sunk nearby. Their home was searched, they were ordered to move away from the coastline, and forbidden to live in Cornwall. When the Lawrences moved to London from Zennor, and later to Lawrence's sister's home in the Midlands, they were homeless, nearly penniless, and were forced into begging friends for places to stay. In London, they were again placed under surveillance. Lawrence was bereft because he had loved living in Zennor; but he was furious too. One of the great tragedies of his life was being forced to leave Cornwall. While there, he wrote, "At last I am in my own home and feel content. I feel I have a place here."

The expulsion, according to Lawrence's biographer John Worthen, changed him and how he regarded the nature of home for the rest of his life. He now called himself an exile, comparing himself to "Ovid in Thrace." He also called himself an outsider, a pirate, a highwayman, an outlaw, a fox in a den. He said he liked "not to have a home," that he enjoyed a nomadic existence and felt "a real panic" if he was "on the brink of taking another house." A permanent abode, he believed, would be "a log on my ankle." Frieda, though, believed that these remarks were inauthentic, a result of their being forced into an unwanted exile, which, she said, changed Lawrence utterly: his wonder and joy at the world vanished.

After these two events, Lawrence believed he could no longer live in England. Still, when they first left, he felt leaving was "a form of death." Forever after, Lawrence felt rootless, often homeless, though he professed to love the nomadic life. The only real world for him, he maintained, was his "inner soul."

Lawrence came to believe eradicating property ownership was necessary for the world to become a better place. He connected the "love of property" with the "love of power," believing if he owned a house he would "become wicked." Possessions "sticking on me like barnacles" made him feel destructive, he said. Often, they would leave behind their household goods, set out with a knapsack, his "kitchenino"—a contraption rigged to make tea and light meals on the road—and head to someplace else, furnishing their new household with items from jumble shops, furnishings he made himself, objects begged from friends.

There were times he realized his restlessness was a symptom of inner disquiet: "What ails me I don't know, but it's on and on." Frieda, though, always "craved a home and solidity," and their arguments often resembled those of Lawrence's parents about living arrangements.

A friend of the Lawrences once called them "birds of passage." No matter how difficult the circumstances, wherever Lawrence was—the home of a friend, an inn, a hotel, a steamer, a rented villa—he set up house and immediately began work. After Frieda and he were forced to leave Cornwall, after their stay in London and while living in his sister's rented house in the Midlands, Lawrence completed his essays on American literature. On a steamer to Ceylon, he translated Verga's *Mastro-don Gesualdo*. In a rented bungalow in the resort of Thirroul in New South Wales, Australia, he began his novel *Kangaroo* and wrote three thousand words a day for six weeks straight, using the people he met and the landscape he witnessed in his work. Although he could work anyplace, he didn't seem to feel at home anywhere, and this troubled him. But he believed it freed him too.

Lawrence drew upon the places he lived and the people he knew for his subject matter. His art was intensely autobiographical. He manifested an extraordinary capacity to render the places he moved to and the people he met in exquisite detail, often satirically. He was a keen observer, alert to the gestures in human behavior signifying character. It's almost as if he moved from one place to another to gather material. He used his experiences more as fodder for his art than as moments to be experienced for their own inherent value.

Lawrence discovered his powers of observation became keener in a new place. After a time, he ceased to "see" where he lived and the dullness of familiarity set in. Once his vision became blunted by habit and routine, he moved on. The source of Lawrence's inspiration seemed tied to novelty and change.

Lawrence often used where he lived as a setting for his work, transforming the people he met into characters, plucking a life situation to examine, conceptualizing a creative work, and beginning it. Moving often gave him new material, allowing another work to germinate. Sometimes he worked on a project in situ—as when he began *Kangaroo* in Australia. But often he wrote about a place when he no longer lived there—as when he wrote *Sons and Lovers*. After he moved away from them, his settings took on a mythic quality, becoming remembered places. That sense of one's continuing connection to a lost place through its re-creation in memory is often an important component of his art.

Lawrence moved too because he alienated the people he wrote about. His work was intensely critical of people's behavior. He said his mission was to describe people's faults and wrongful ways so they would improve themselves, never doubting he knew what was wrong with them and how they should change. He used the scalpel of words to lay bare each of his character's foibles, illusions, hypocrisies. What he did, he knew, was "write bombs."

Except when he was forced to move from Cornwall, Lawrence looked forward to relocating, to setting up house again. Once Frieda and he had hatched a plan to move, he was optimistic, full of hope that this new place would be the "Promised Land" and that he would feel freer and more at peace there. When he thought about the advantages of a new place, he idealized it and studied its history. When he dreamed of living in Erice in Sicily, he thought about the ancient Greek settlement there. It seemed the only places worth settling in were those connected with history, for they would allow him "a most fascinating act of self-discovery—back, back down the old ways of time." But Lawrence understood, too, that any place would come to dissatisfy him, enrage him; it seemed fascinating when he imagined it, and its reality could never live up to his expectations.

Lawrence believed human beings were not stagnant by nature but infinitely capable of change. The easiest way to change, he believed, was to move. As he grew older, he became committed to constant change, and one of the most powerful insults he could hurl at a person was that they were static. "The human being is a most curious creature," he wrote. "He thinks he has got one soul, and he has got dozens." Moving back to Taormina from Sardinia, Lawrence said that he felt his "Sardinian soul melting off me, I felt myself evaporating into the real Italian uncertainty and momentaneity." The only way to metamorphose from one self into another was to move; the only way to experience all the possible selves one could be was to move often.

But Lawrence did not believe everyone should move. He

believed some, like Paulo, a man he met in San Gaudenzio in Italy, ought to stay where they were born; these were the "authentic" souls Lawrence wanted to encounter on his peregrinations. Paulo had moved to America, and to Lawrence "his going away was an excursion from reality, a kind of sleep-walking. He left his own reality in the soil. . . . But the very quick of him was killed."

At the beginning of Lawrence's *The Sea and Sardinia*, which is as much about moving as it is about Sardinia, Lawrence asks, "Why can't one sit still?"—meaning, "Why can't I sit still?" He wondered why, even when he lived in Taormina where life was "so pleasant," he journeyed to Sardinia looking for a still better place to live. He knew it made no sense, for moving was inconvenient and drained their already meager resources. Lawrence answers his question in a way that helps illuminate his motives—and many other people's—for wanting to move.

Lawrence's initial answer is that we undertake a move because we anticipate the pleasure it will give us. But then he realizes "it is the motion of freedom" he's after. If he lives in one place a long time, he feels fettered. Moving makes him feel like a free spirit, bound to no domicile, no set of people, no community, no country.

Still, when he contemplated settling in Sardinia permanently, he rejected the idea because the place had began to dissatisfy him. Because it didn't meet his expectations, he was enraged: it "had seemed so fascinating to me when I imagined it beforehand," he said. Again it could not meet his idealized vision.

In writing *The Sea and Sardinia*, Lawrence learned that many of his moves were impelled by anger; whenever he began to feel enraged, he moved on. The village of Sorgono seemed to hold much promise. Frieda and he liked the sound of its name, felt "Sorgono . . . will be lovely" and they might linger there awhile. Soon after arriving, though, Lawrence became outraged. His mood became "black, black, black" because an innkeeper didn't make a fire quickly enough and was vague about the time for supper. Frieda chided Lawrence that a great fault of his was that he couldn't take life as it came because he expected it to be other than it was. He conceded that "Sorgono had seemed so fascinating" but didn't meet his expectations, so he became disappointed, furious, and decided to move to Nuoro instead.

Lawrence often ascribed his rage to outside circumstances. Sometimes, as when he and Frieda were expelled from Cornwall, his fury was appropriate because they had been mistreated. Often, though, as when they left Sorgono, his rage was awakened because a place did not meet his expectations and Lawrence blamed the place, not his unrealistic view of what he'd find there. Though Lawrence also understood his fury was often unwarranted and an overreaction to some event, this insight didn't cause him to try to control his rage, work through it, and stay put. Instead, it dictated his behavior. He seemed to relish his anger while it lasted, even as he felt impelled to move away from the place where he experienced it. Perhaps he knew that if he stayed put, he might harm someone—his anger was that unpredictable and dangerous. Perhaps leaving a place protected Lawrence from what he feared he might do while there. He could become violent, as Katherine Mansfield witnessed when she lived near the Lawrences in Cornwall; the Lawrences often assaulted each other, and Mansfield had seen the marks of Lawrence's physical abuse on Frieda's body and had heard about Frieda's blows.

But Lawrence also knew "he didn't feel angry while travelling." On his sea voyage to Ceylon, he remarked, "No more of my tirades—the sea seems too big." Contemplating an ever-changing novel seascape or landscape made Lawrence focus his attention outside himself, which acted as balm to his troubled spirit. After arriving somewhere, settling down, and setting up house, the demons of dissatisfaction, disillusionment, dis-ease, and rage would come visiting. And soon, with a knapsack and the kitchenino, Frieda and he would be off to another place, where the cycle would repeat itself.

Ceylon was no exception. The Lawrences set up house in Ceylon, as always, with very little furniture—"chairs and a table or two"—but for the first time, with servants. He soon started writing, composing the poem "The Elephant," based on a ritual he had observed. Still, he believed he would not write a great deal while there because the people he met didn't work—"one doesn't do much here, I tell you," he observed in a letter to his sister Emily. Because they didn't work, he believed he wouldn't work, and he needed to work because he had promised his publisher he would transform his experience in Ceylon into a novel.

The circumstances under which he was living, he complained, weren't conducive to creativity. The heat was oppressive and simply moving his body caused him to sweat; he developed stomach trouble and dysentery; the smells and food of the place made him nauseated; "the horrid noises of the birds and creatures [of the forest], who hammer and clang and rattle and cackle and explode all the livelong day" outraged him, especially because he couldn't make them stop. He expected Ceylon to be a "new start." He conceded that it was "rather fascinating, but I don't know how long we shall stay."

But there was this too: Lawrence felt he was suffocating in Ceylon. He described "the thick, choky feel of tropical forest," wrote that it felt like "a real prison." He needed to "get out." Several of Lawrence's moves were made—and the one from Ceylon was among them—because he was forever searching for a place where he could breathe more easily.

Miserable, unsettled, unable to breathe easily, Lawrence became repulsed by Ceylon. He regretted the move, believing Frieda and he had made a huge mistake leaving Europe. Looking around at the strange landscape, he felt untethered, uprooted, not quite himself. "I . . . sort of look round for myself among all this different world," he wrote, and acknowledged he was "running away."

The Lawrences left Ceylon six weeks after arriving and moved to Australia. After they decided to leave Ceylon, Lawrence admitted, "I like the feeling of rolling on." And, with characteristic insight he added, "I love trying things and discovering how I hate them."

SEVEN

"A Door, Opening"

Changing Lives

A SEASON OUT OF TIME . . .

The poet and memoirist Mark Doty's childhood was nomadic. He felt "absolutely, plainly alone" because of all the moves his family made—seven in seven years by the time he was in second grade, and many thereafter. Doty's father worked with the Army Corps of Engineers, necessitating the family's constant relocations. Still, Doty wonders what other reasons might have accounted for his father's restlessness.

Because of his peripatetic childhood, Doty wanted to put down roots as an adult, become part of a community, find a true home and "cultivate it and keep it." After he and his lover Wally Roberts moved to Provincetown, Massachusetts, Doty thought he had found where he would live for the rest of his life. He believed that his mother's alcoholism was a consequence of his family's constant moves and that settling down was essential for his own emotional well-being.

After each move, his mother, a painter, would work hard at learning the ways of a new community, making friends, turning their house into a home. Then she would have to leave, sever her connections, pack up, move on to a new place, and start all over. Each move entailed irreconcilable losses; each left her feeling sadder and more isolated than before, resulting in her emotional disintegration.

One move in particular—one that took her away from a beloved home in the desert landscape of Tucson, Arizona, to a nondescript house in the suburbs in Titusville, Florida—made her condition far worse. After this move, as Doty writes in his memoir *Firebird*, it was like "she turned some corner, . . . and ceased to be willing to start again."

All her adult life, his mother had a recurring dream she shared with her son, which warned Doty of living a nomadic life. It is the quintessential dream of wanting to settle down but being forced by circumstances to keep moving.

"It's night in a strange city," Doty writes, retelling his mother's dream. "She's walking, and suddenly she realizes she has no idea where in the world she is. No matter how long and how far she walks, there's nothing familiar, nothing to give her any clue; this street resembles a block in that city, but as soon as she thinks she knows where she might be something else contradicts it. How did she get here, and where is the here she's gotten to? The doors don't open, the streets don't turn onto any known corner, any landmark of home. And when she wakes she's just as panicked, just as lost, till she remembers where she is."

Still, Doty finds that despite the negative effect of a transient life on his mother, he too sometimes feels compelled to move and believes there exists within each of us "a fierce internal debate, between staying moored and drifting away, between holding on and letting go." This, he says, is part of the human condition. "Wisdom lies in our ability to negotiate between these two poles," he concludes: to know when to stay rooted and when to move away—and to accept the pull of each drive without harming oneself in the process. "Permanence, stability, rootedness" is what Doty values, although he is "always fleeing it too." And his flight is often prompted by knowing that to change, he must move on.

Heaven's Coast, a memoir about Doty's relationship with Wally, his lover and partner of twelve years, chronicles the pair's move to Provincetown, what that place signified to them both, the changes in Doty's work while there, and Wally's death.

Doty and Wally first lived together in a Boston neighborhood of "brownstones and brick rowhouses, iron fences, and lampposts." They then moved to Vermont, but often returned to Boston for doctor's appointments, "for a badly needed dose of urbanity and style," or to see what they could enjoy there "now." Although they continued to enjoy Boston, they hurried back home, realizing they'd changed and city life no longer suited them. They were happy they didn't live "in the speed and abrasion" of the city anymore.

After Wally died, Doty made a ritual trip to Boston. He walked down Charles Street, past Romano's bakery, where they would go for pastries, to the Public Gardens with their trees, pond, and swan boats. He recalled how, here, Wally and he had moved from "being 'in love' to living in love, which is quite a different thing." No other place they lived would ever "hold quite the resonance" of Boston, for it had become "so emblematic and so completely interiorized, the city surface transformed into the surface of dream." This happens when significant changes in our lives occur in certain places. After we leave, they become places "of rapture and longing and wonder," like "the portico of a church—little private space," remembers Doty, where "we'd duck inside to kiss, happy transgression."

On this memorial trip, Doty gained access to a little studio apartment at 115 Beacon Street where he'd lived. When he entered, he felt as if he were "opening the gates of a tomb." The person he was while living there no longer existed. Visiting a former home charts how much we have changed through time. Still, the man he was then came back to him in memory—"gloriously alive," passionately in love, adventurous about plunging headlong into this "risky adventurous union."

Before meeting Wally, Doty had left a failed heterosexual marriage and moved from the Midwest, where "gay people were hidden, erased," to New York. His move to the East could be summarized, he said, by the words "Young Gay Man Leaves Stultifying Midwest for the Urban World of Romance and Permission." In New York, he didn't have to hide his sexuality.

He came to New York with only six hundred dollars and struggled to find a job and an affordable apartment. In the city, he worked as a typist for as many hours as he could. His life was "more about survival than pleasure."

On a rare holiday, he went to Bellows Falls, Vermont, stayed at a gay hotel, met Wally, and thought, *Here you are at last.* After three months, Doty moved from New York to Boston, where Wally had a "more established life" than Doty did. But after Doty arrived, Wally thought it might be too soon to live together, so Doty rented that small studio on Beacon Street, in the building where Wally lived in a large apartment.

After their relationship grew more settled, Doty got a grant from the Massachusetts Artists Foundation, which they used as a down payment for a house in Montpelier, Vermont. It was a "ramshackle" thirteen-room Italianate Victorian situated in a hollow at the base of a hill. It was built in 1884, most likely for housing men who worked in a nearby granite quarry. The house was ugly—it was painted mustard yellow with chocolate-colored trim—and it had been poorly maintained. The property was enclosed with a rickety picket fence, also painted brown.

The Realtor who showed them the house told them they should tear it down and build another on the land. But being "contrary creatures," they bought the place for twenty-four thousand dollars and decided to restore it. Its floor plan had been altered into "a carnival maze." Its only source of heat was a wood-burning furnace; it had no insulation; the stove burned kerosene; its ancient plumbing needed replacing; the flat roof leaked and required shoveling during heavy snowstorms. But they discovered its linoleum concealed wide-plank floors. The house had possibilities, and what mattered was that this "great rambling dream of a house, eccentric, temperamental, rife with character, [was] capable of being profoundly loved."

They now owned a "piece of the world on which to make our mark." They had visions of how they would rescue this house, transform it, inhabit it, play with it, and play in it. For five years, they "painted and plastered and stripped and cursed, built and caulked and wept." All their spare money went into fixing the house. They painted the exterior a creamy colonial yellow with white trim and blue shutters. They fixed the roof and the chimney, bought storm doors, built a new picket fence and painted it white, planted and tended a garden with lilies, monkshood, delphinium, campanula, strawflowers, love-in-a-mist. Wally, who earned his living as a window designer, had a particular flair for decorating the house with auction finds—a green stepback cupboard; a wooden panel painted with wild birds; a huge oak table; a glass ball; a yellow chest of drawers; a cream-colored chair.

Even castoffs like an unfinished violin and a broken blue and white china platter decorated with a group of deer looked just right where he placed them.

Through making this house into their home, Doty and Wally solidified their commitment to their relationship. They believed they would live here for years. When they bought the house, they'd looked forward to enjoying it. Yet it required so much of their labor there was barely time for pleasure. As soon as they completed one project, another needed to be undertaken; then something that had been repaired years before needed fixing again. There was, too, the ongoing, never-ending work of the garden. Though arduous, Doty believed gardening anchored him: "It held me in place."

Then Wally was diagnosed as HIV-positive.

In the emotional aftermath of receiving the diagnosis, Doty and Wally bought a cabin on six wooded acres in Vermont only thirty miles from their home. It was bordered by a state forest and a marsh. Buying the cabin wasn't "sensible," they knew. But it was "about longing." Doty loved the marsh and the woods; Wally, though, felt isolated there. They soon realized the cabin was Doty's passion, not Wally's. And Doty realized that their impulsive decision to buy it represented "another life, another set of possibilities" to them, which eased the pain of knowing that their future would be vastly different from times past.

Doty imagined the cabin would bring a sense of safety and tranquility into their lives during this troubled time. But it did not. "Wally's attention," Doty knew, "was elsewhere." He would have to let the cabin go. Now, neither of them could know "what sort of change was coming," but they knew it was "gathering speed, establishing direction."

Doty learned an essential lesson from owning the house in

Montpelier and the cabin: "What a fragile thing a house is," he said, "though it doesn't seem so." These places could not provide him with stability because of Wally's illness. Doty was forced to learn a life lesson about the impermanence of all things—a house, a lover, himself. He learned that everything changes: "Paint peels, plaster cracks, and gardens, of course, are the most ephemeral constructions of all." This realization helped him through Wally's illness.

Doty's shift in perspective made him acutely aware of how any order we make in our lives can "vanish so quickly." He began to look at the world "through a glass tinted with the awareness of mortality." Doty and Wally believed they had rescued the house. But all they'd done was to make it "not merely habitable but lovely" for a time. "The gleam of a loved house," Doty wrote, "lasts only as long as he who loves it can keep polishing." For a time, Wally and he had turned that house into "a dwelling place, a deeply occupied zone in which to encounter and to recapitulate all our dwellings, a house deep enough, ours enough, to dream into. And then time swept us away, and in time took the house itself."

Doty and Wally decided they needed to move from Vermont to a place that was congenial to a gay man living with HIV and his partner, one where each could find support and where Wally could receive excellent medical care. They now needed a community where others understood their situation because they too had experienced it. Had they stayed in Vermont, they would have been "sealed together in some kind of bubble, a private sphere." Although they needed to move, Doty also "wanted" to move. Still, the thought of leaving his garden made Doty feel he was leaving "some irreplaceable part of the history of my heart."

But once the decision was made, Doty felt energized. Wally

and he had chosen "moving ahead," no matter how frightening the future. They no longer postponed making decisions nor deferred indulging themselves. They were now forced to think about how they'd best spend the limited time they had together. With the move, they started to feel their "way toward change."

Before selling the house in Vermont, Doty and Wally moved—temporarily, they believed—to Provincetown, to a "rented cottage on a strip of beach at the farthest narrow crook of land" at the very tip of the Cape. The year they moved, the weather was mild, and the place quickly became the refuge Doty had sought during this difficult time. Working at his desk, watching Wally and their dog Arden sitting on a low dune on the beach beside the house, Doty believed they had been given a great gift, "a season out of time." Watching the constantly changing sea was an enormous comfort; it was all flux and change, never appearing "remotely similar" to the way it looked before.

Provincetown also turned out to have a surprising connection with Doty's family history. His ancestor Edward Dotey was a passenger on the *Mayflower*, which landed in Provincetown before moving on to Plymouth. Dotey was a scoundrel who probably took the journey to escape debtor's prison in England. He seemed to have been cast out of the colony, and he died on the Cape. Doty was unaware of this story when he first moved in, but his rented house was on the exact spot where his ancestor, "370 years before, had probably been among the sixteen armed men who first rode a longboat into shore from *The Mayflower*." He had fallen in love with the very landscape his ancestor had witnessed.

Doty and Wally celebrated this connection by visiting a replica of the *Mayflower* and by attending a reenactment of the landing. For the first time, Doty felt "particularly American, embedded in American history, here at the nation's slender tip."

Initially, living in Provincetown was far easier than living in Vermont. Being so near the sea made Wally's illness seem "far away." Here their life was "brighter, less freighted," than it had been. They realized how much hard work the old Montpelier place required to keep it from falling apart. They had more free time and enjoyed themselves more and realized they didn't want to—couldn't—go back to a life so work-filled. Once, after a short trip, Doty returned to the Cape and felt, "I'm home now." He'd experienced a "new sense of an arrival, a door in my life opening."

Their rented house in Provincetown was old, built perhaps in 1790. There, Wally became very ill once, and Doty and he began to wonder how many people who'd lived there had become ill, how many had died in these rooms during the past two centuries. Knowing that Wally would die, Doty realized he was living in a "highly provisional . . . stability." He would cherish those times when he felt relatively at peace. "No one," he said, "can live in endless uncertainty."

Provincetown seemed like "a balm," welcoming them; here, they were just another ordinary couple. Being HIV-positive in Provincetown wasn't unusual, and this was comforting. Until moving to Provincetown, Doty did not realize how "*watched*" he'd felt in Vermont.

Doty and Wally soon wanted a more permanent home in Provincetown and decided to buy a house before they had to vacate their rental. They bought the first house they looked at; as soon as they saw it, they fell in love. It was a small two-hundred-year-old house in the "distinctive Cape Cod style," just a block away from the harbor. They wanted an old house because "real beauty," Doty said, "is always marked by the passage of time; . . . its loveliness increases as the workings of age and the mysteries of continuing enhance it."

When they inspected the house, they discovered a fireplace in a neglected bedroom upstairs; it was nearly papered over but surrounded by eighteenth-century beaded boards. This made them realize there were probably more hidden treasures, and in time, they discovered three more fireplaces. Doty especially liked that the house "looked hunkered down against a storm"; during its long life, it had indeed withstood many storms.

Making this house into a true refuge became a project for them while Wally was still strong. In Vermont, their tasks seemed endless because the Montpelier house was so big; here, their work was limited and doable. First, they researched its history, learning it was probably floated to Provincetown from Truro. They discovered local documents showing the house's original appearance. They made detailed plans for restoration and improvements—jacking up sagging floors; sanding and refinishing them; rebuilding rotting eaves and crumbling sills; stripping away vinyl paneling and gypsum; stripping the old wood.

As they worked, they discovered "the sturdy and simple bones of a beautiful house: hemlock beams in the low ceilings, intimate little rooms with walls of a soft plaster made of sand and horsehair and oyster shells." They felt "new reserves of energy" as they returned the house to its original character; they knew their restoration was adding something valuable to a community they loved. Doty designed and planted a garden appropriate to the Cape landscape, and together they built a picket fence to enclose it. They were rewarded with a bloom of huge roses during their first summer.

Moving into this history-infused house made Doty and Wally reexamine their lives; theirs, too, were "part of history" and now, a part of the history of this house. As Wally's condition worsened, as Doty rubbed his feet to ease his pain, Wally wondered whether the spirits of those who had lived here would "come and stand around him." Though Wally's grave illness was a sobering reality, nonetheless, the house's solidity, the "gravity of the big beams holding the roof down," made Doty understand that "the will to inhabit, to make, out of whatever is offered, a dwelling place," is a "contagious persistence" in the lives of all human beings.

After Wally's death, images from their life together before his condition worsened consoled Doty: "Our green and brown bicycles. . . . My garden trowel and spade. . . . Wally's handsome bow ties. . . . The mantel newly painted a licheny gray-green. . . . Lovely rough antique hardware. . . . A heavy glass vase full of pink and white cosmos, which bloomed and bloomed. A jar of paste wax, for the old oak dining table."

Despite the difficulty of Wally's long illness, Doty learned nonetheless "to be fully *in* our lives," though often he "could hardly bear to look" at what was happening. This acceptance depended somehow, he believed, on their move to Provincetown and this particular house. Love and desire, he learned, have "less to do with possession" and more to do with "participation, the will to involve oneself in the body of the world" wherever we find ourselves, under whatever circumstances: "a lover's irreplaceable body, the roil and shimmer of sea overshot with sunlight, a handful of cherries, the texture and weight of a word." In Provincetown, he was strong enough to be the "witness" of his lover's dying, recording what it was he saw and experienced, even though it was "unbearable." But "*not* to look," not to write, was also unbearable.

Witness and recount he did, providing a no-holds-barred description of Wally's life during the nine months he was confined to bed: the pleasure of a foot rub, a sponge bath; the "matter

of shit" that became "a new fact of life"; Wally's new food crav-
ings; how Wally slid onto the floor and Doty hurt himself trying
to lift his deadweight by himself; the surprising sexual desire that
surfaced in Wally during his last months and his joy at the beautiful men passing outside his window; the last surprise birthday
party; the insertion of a catheter; the loss of language; Wally's loss
of the use of his hands; the last Christmas present of fleece-lined
slippers decorated with images of bacon and eggs; Wally's turning
inward and letting go.

Finally—but not finally at all, for the moment has never left
him—Doty recorded the time of Wally's dying, when he felt "the
movement of energy, the *leap* of spirit, lifting from him." Doty
then became "a citizen of grief's country." In time, after scattering
Wally's ashes in the nearby marsh they both loved, something
within Doty shifted, however, although "one does not lose—one
does not *want* to lose, entirely—grief." Now he felt "Wally's body
belong[ed] in the huge sun-burnished field of the salt marsh." It
was the first image Doty saw whenever he arrived in Provincetown,
or left.

Whether their move to Provincetown lengthened Wally's
life, Doty couldn't say. But he knows their remaining years together were far "brighter" than they would have been elsewhere.

After Wally's death, Provincetown changed for Doty, becoming synonymous with the mystery of mortality—dying, death,
transcendence. Through the years, he had mined Provincetown's
poetic potential in his work. It existed as a borderland between
land and sea representing so many other junctures in his life,
as the title of his memoir—*Heaven's Coast*—indicates. After Wally's
death, Doty's understanding of the metaphoric richness of this place
deepened.

Provincetown, because it is on the sea, with a great swath of sky visible, became emblematic of Doty's belief that everything is in a state of constant change. In addition to being a border between land and sea, Provincetown also signified "a border town between worlds," the land of the living and that "unknowable, impenetrable" place of death. On his beach walks, Doty began noticing seal carcasses, a dolphin skeleton; the beach became "an arena of mortality, corpses washing in and out, the consequences of predation or pollution or exposure." But though death seemed an "utter, unbearable rupture," living in Provincetown taught Doty that death is also "kind."

A DEEP SILENCE . . .

After Wally's death in 1994, Doty continued to live in the home they shared. In time, another man came into his life, the novelist and memoirist Paul Lisicky, who moved in with him. They lived there for ten more years, during which Provincetown remained an "ideal place." But Provincetown changed during those ten years. An influx of wealthy people bought summer homes, and the village became gentrified and lost much of its raffish charm. Dissatisfied with life there, Doty and Lisicky decided to look for another, more suitable place to live.

Once they decided to move, they realized they'd been romanticizing Provincetown for some time: it no longer was the place it had been. They learned that if you don't remain alert to how you feel about where you live, you might linger there longer than you should. For Doty, Provincetown was where he grieved Wally's death and the death of two beloved dogs. He now wanted to find a place without that sorrowful history so he could enter a new period in his emotional and creative life.

One period in his writing life had ended, and the confluence of meanings he'd derived from living in Provincetown had been exhausted. "The way I could find what I needed there, in terms of metaphor," he said, "had come to an end." Moving elsewhere would provide him with a whole new landscape to contemplate, a whole new set of images for his poetry, a whole new range of over-arching metaphors to explain his soul's work at this new stage of his life. There would be another, different landscape to experience and reflect upon.

Doty's relationship to landscape has always been profound. He knew he now wanted a house with an ideal relationship to its landscape, one in which the house's architecture related to its sur-roundings. When his family moved to a house in Tucson, Ari-zona, in a desert landscape, his mother's creative work as a painter changed; for the first time the landscape spoke to her "deeply." Suddenly, there was a "flowering of desire to fill page and canvas with form and color." She was inspired by the desert's "shift of light and shadow, blue and gold, the soft austerity of arroyo and foothill and mountain." In *Firebird*, Doty observes, "When you love a place enough, it seems almost to be inside you, as if it were the physical equivalent of an inner life." With Lisicky, Doty searched for a new place that might likewise shift his own way of seeing the world.

Doty and Lisicky found just such a place on New York's Fire Island. Again, it was the first house Doty visited. It wasn't an old house, but "a 1960s contemporary ranch" in the Pines, very differ-ent from his historic home in Provincetown. It, too, though, had been a "floater," taken to the island by boat.

The landscape first attracted them, seeming to promise what Doty and Lisicky both felt they now needed in their creative lives: the solitude to do their work. Whereas Provincetown provided a community, Fire Island is a place for them to "hide out and write, and to regroup," as Lisicky has stated. What Doty now needs, and what he's found (except on summer weekends), is a "silence, . . . deeper than just about anywhere."

Whereas the house in Cape Cod felt like a protected "winter" house to hunker down in, the Fire Island house, with vaulted ceilings, white beams, sliding glass doors, and clerestory windows flooding the house with light, invites the outdoors in. The furnishings they have chosen for this house are very different from those in Provincetown: modern sofas, Eames chairs, a glass table, objects found on the beach. But there are things brought from Provincetown too—a B&B sign, old bookshelves—reminders of their connection to that beloved place.

The house in the Pines reminds both Lisicky and Doty of former homes: Lisicky's family's summer cottage in Ocean City, New Jersey, and one of Doty's Tucson homes, the one close to the desert where his mother was happiest and painted her boldest works—it, too, had a room with a cathedral ceiling and floor-to-ceiling and clerestory windows, and felt as if it were a part of the landscape; from the backyard, he could "look right up into the smoke-blue heaven of the Santa Catalina mountains."

On Fire Island, Doty is working on a garden, different from those he's previously cultivated. Here, there are blue hydrangeas, orange daylilies, and fuchsia peonies. Working in his garden is a continuation of his past life, although it also represents his new and different life on Fire Island.

A SABBATH . . .

One afternoon about a month after moving, I pick up Sara Jenkins's *This Side of Nirvana*, a book about the impediments to her Buddhist practice. She writes about her restlessness and how it had driven her to move whenever she felt discomfort. She describes how she finally settled down and acquired a house, furniture, pets, and a car, and how this brought a necessary "ballast" to her life. Only after deciding to settle down could she come to terms with what "can only be learned in the process of sticking it out through the discomfort."

Yes, I too have been feeling discomfort in this house. And instead of acknowledging it, of staying with it, I've run out on it again and again. I haven't met the house on its own terms; haven't let it tell me how to live here. Like Jenkins, I must pay attention to the house and let it guide me, let it tell me about what kind of life might best be lived here.

Jenkins decided that in her new home she would engage in the observance of a "Sabbath" to see if it would calm her continuing feelings of restlessness. On her Sabbath, she would "make no social engagements, unplug the telephone, do no work, and spend the day in quiet and simple pleasures."

I decide to see what will happen if I stay at home for my own "Sabbath." And although it is difficult at first, in time I look forward to this day that I spend with the house, doing nothing but existing within it. And so slowly I let myself become the person the house seems to want me to be. A woman who has chosen to become more private, to turn her back on much of public life, to become more solitary, quieter, slower, a woman who is surprised by the person she is becoming. A woman who spends more time knitting than reading. One who makes simple soups from vegetables and heirloom beans she collects instead of the fancy food she used to spend hours concocting. One who is content to wander through the house at various times of day to watch how the light falls across a carpet, illuminating a speck of green she has never seen before. A woman who writes very little in her journal because she is mesmerized by the birds coming to the tiny waterfall in her backyard to drink and by the red-tailed hawk with a nest high up in a tree two houses over alighting on a branch who might at any moment swoop down to grab one of these birds in its talons for a meal.

For now, though, the hawk seems content to perch and survey. Perhaps it is satiated; or perhaps it will feed a little later, after I have moved away from the window. But it is in the moment that I see the hawk and realize that this wild thing inhabits the same space I do, that I turn the corner on my feelings of loss and tell myself, "Yes, this place is my home."

I WILL WRITE HERE . . .

In 1930, Henry Miller arrived in Paris alone, without his second wife, June, to pursue his dream of becoming a published writer. He arrived with a trunk and two suitcases containing custom-made suits tailored by his father, which he planned to sell if he needed money, a copy of Walt Whitman's *Leaves of Grass*, manuscripts of two unpublished novels written during the past six years—*Moloch* (about his first marriage and his job at Western Union) and *Crazy Cock* (about his marriage to June and her lesbian love affair, the thought of which still plagued him). He had only ten dollars in cash, money he had borrowed from his best friend, Emil Schnellock, enough for just a few days. June had promised she'd wire him money, so he spent part of each day on a "dreary walk to the American Express office" on rue Scribe hoping he would find a money order, but suspecting "there would be no mail for me, no check, no cable, nothing, nothing." Although he knew he needed to be alone to write, Miller hoped June would surprise him with a visit. But in the early days of his stay in Paris, she never sent a note or funds.

In his fiction, Miller recalls "the splendor of those miserable days when I first arrived in Paris, a bewildered, poverty-stricken individual who haunted the streets like a ghost at a banquet." Still, there was something cleansing and life-altering about the experience, "a weird sort of contentment." For he had "no appointments, no invitations for dinner, no program, no dough." He began to refer to this time as "the golden period," when his view of life and of what was important to him changed utterly. He learned to live moment to moment, to expect nothing, to hope for the best.

It was June who suggested the move and who funded his passage. Miller was surprised, but agreed. The story the Millers told each other was that Henry was moving to Europe to "write a novel that would make him famous and establish her as one of the muses of the ages." Which is essentially what happened, although by the time this occurred, the Millers were separated. Later, he learned that June's apparent generosity was prompted because she wanted Miller out of the way. She was involved with another man, Stratford Corbett, an insurance agent, whose prospects seemed better than Henry's. Henry hadn't yet produced the masterpiece, starring her as heroine, she'd awaited. Most likely it was Corbett's money that paid for Henry's passage. After the Millers divorced, June married Corbett.

Miller had agreed to the separation because he wanted to finish a novel that would earn him the recognition he sought, and which so far had eluded him. He was in his thirties, and it was now or never, he believed, and he was finding it more and more impossible to work around June. Or, rather, he was finding it more and

more difficult to endure her absences from home, her erratic behavior, and the cockamamie excuses she gave him.

Although he missed June terribly and was unbearably lonely
without her, he learned that if he was to survive, he would have
to learn to nourish himself *"from within."* His early days in Paris
made him discover that "what the artist needs is *loneliness."* To
quell his emotional pain, Miller decided to make Paris his new
lover, to find out everything he could about the city, to examine
it block by block, arrondissement by arrondissement. He would
learn why Paris was special, discover what Paris could mean to
him, ponder what kind of writer he wanted to become here.

He found the homes where famous writers like Balzac, Eu-
gène Sue, Rousseau, Baudelaire, Cervantes, Villon, and Victor
Hugo had lived. He learned how each quarter differed and what
its special attractions were—"the animated elegance of the
champs Elysees"; "the working-class pigments of the vegetable
market at Les Halles." He met the photographer Brassaï, "the eye
of Paris," then in the early stages of his career, and helped him
carry his equipment. Years later, Miller said that "when you suffer
somewhere and you can't escape, you begin to accept the situation and then you find marvelous things in it." In the midst of his
poverty, Miller "discovered Paris" and "got to love it." The most
important aspect about his early days in Paris, he said, was being
"without anything, no crutch of any kind," which forced him into
living "from day to day," and made him exultant about his ability
to survive.

Henry and June had visited Paris two years before, in 1928.
Their trip had been financed by a man—probably one of
June's "sugar daddies"—who gave her money to go to Europe
to write a novel. The benefactor, not knowing she was married,
gave June about two thousand dollars, enough money to last

her—them—almost a year in Paris. The deal was that, in exchange, she would have a finished novel in hand upon her return that she'd let him read. He assumed the novel would be titillating.

June was no writer. She had been a "taxi dancer"—a woman who worked in a dance hall—and quite likely a prostitute when Henry met her in New York City. After they married, Henry wrote some work and passed it off as hers, hoping that something penned by a beautiful woman would be easier to sell. As part of the Paris con, Miller gave his novel *Crazy Cock*, the novel about June's lesbian love affair, to June to present to her benefactor as if it were her own.

And off they went, with Miller hoping that he could become the well-recognized writer he dreamed of becoming while living in Paris.

Miller was excited when they arrived at Gare St.-Lazare, "with its glassed-in roof and the big waiting room called . . . 'The Hall of Lost Footsteps,'" the place where so many people had said their good-byes. The significance of this name was not lost on him, though: his marriage to June was tenuous and he knew she might leave him, as she had before.

The Millers moved into the Grand Hotel de la France on rue Bonaparte. Henry, who knew no French, consulted his dictionary to make their needs known.

After a few weeks, Henry and June became "fed up with cathedrals and squares" and decided to bicycle through France. Henry, who was a superb cyclist, taught his femme fatale wife June how to ride, but her idea of activity was to tramp around Greenwich Village in the early hours of the morning wearing dramatic capes and masklike makeup.

They rode from Paris to Marseilles, fighting furiously en route. They often ate picnic lunches—"a hunk of salami, some

French bread, cheese and fruit"—to economize, although June was not a frugal woman, and the last place you'd expect to find her was at a picnic. Away from the demimonde of New York, away from the nightlife of Paris, she was out of her element. Cycling through France, watching June in her inappropriate clothing riding ahead of him, Henry began to understand they were no longer compatible. He was changing; he was serious about becoming a writer, which is what June had said she wanted of him—only she didn't want to be the partner of a man whose work was so sedentary and self-involved. She wanted a "good time Charlie," not a man serious about his work.

On this trip, the rift between them widened. Here, there were no men whom June could seduce into providing her with money, no female lover who would fawn over her; no diversions from her relationship with Henry. Here, there were no male friends who would help Henry handle his rage at June's behavior; there was no writing to help him understand his pain. On this trip, June was at her worst, Henry said, in the midst of a "delirium of disorder," whether drug-induced or a recurring bout of her mental illness, he could not say. Being with her for days on end, he realized how disturbed she was; he understood how different they were. When they had first met, June's incessant talking had hypnotized him. Now he believed it was the product of a disturbed mind or the effect of too many drugs.

The bicycle trip ended when June had an accident. It marked the death knell of their marriage, although Henry would try to make it work for some time to come.

Just as in New York, June prevented him from working in France, and Miller never touched his notebooks and manuscripts. Much as June professed to be his muse, life with her was too chaotic for him to settle into a writing regimen, which he had to do to fulfill his dream. She wanted him to write a novel with her as its mythic heroine so all the world could understand her appeal and her importance to this man she was sure was a genius. She had taken his writing seriously, had encouraged him to quit his job at Western Union to write; she worked to support him, and for this he was grateful. But on their trip to France, Miller realized June thought his novel would magically appear without much effort on his part. If he wanted to change his life and become a "real" writer, he'd have to leave her.

When Miller first arrived in Paris alone in 1930, he lived the life of a clochard, a man down on his luck. He slept in the Cinéma Vanves (arranged by the ticket taker Eugene Pachoutinsky); in cheap, lice-infested hotels with shredding wallpaper, torn and patched carpets, broken windows; or outside, on the street or under one of Paris's innumerable bridges, with his bundle of manuscripts as a pillow. He sustained himself on "luck, charm, and nerve." A friend remarked that Miller experienced a "poverty that was hungrier than anything I ever heard of." Yet, soon after he arrived, he began writing in a notebook he carried with him everywhere: "I will write here. I will live quietly and alone. And each day I will see a little more of Paris, study it, learn it as I would a book."

He found a modest restaurant off the Place St.-Sulpice, Restaurant des Gourmets, where he could get a meal for forty-eight cents "including wine, butter, bread, serviette and pourbouire." Miller had a magnetic personality and made friends quickly. He began to count on the generosity of Parisians, who didn't regard poverty as a sign of moral failing, and on that of expatriates living in Paris. Although in later life he recounted he'd "lived very poorly" in Paris, there he found a freedom to be himself that he'd never experienced in the United States.

Living in New York, Miller had felt worthless. There, a person's worth was measured by the size of his bank account. Even a rich man could feel poor in New York, and being a working-class man, Miller had scrambled to earn a living as "a street car conductor, garbage collector, librarian, insurance man, book salesman, . . . in a telegraph office, . . . in a mail order house, . . . in the Western Union," never making enough money to make ends meet, prevented from doing the work of his heart full-time because he needed to earn a living, always feeling as if he were living a sham existence. In the United States people were encouraged to "walk the treadmill" to better their circumstances, but even though he was on that treadmill, his circumstances hadn't improved.

Although he had begun writing in New York, he'd never felt any confidence in his ability, nor did people in the United States regard writing as a worthwhile pursuit. In Paris, he was respected for the man he was, not for the position he held or the possessions he owned, which removed the burden of achieving from his shoulders. In Paris, writers were respected whether or not they published and regardless of how much they earned. Although he was often lonely in Paris, he never felt alienated.

In New York, he'd always hoped "some extrinsic event" would alter his life—a better job, more money, a better place to live, a more congenial set of friends—because people living in the United States are urged to believe that chasing money and possessions will make them happy, so they live their lives "in double harness." In Paris, he learned to "expect nothing," to let himself "drift with the tide," but he also learned how to devote himself to the act of writing.

Until Miller met Alfred Perlès and set up house with him in Clichy, Miller was without a home of his own, crashing with people he met, borrowing flats, exchanging his services as a cook and general factotum for lodging, or begging money for lodging and food. He kept careful lists of the money he borrowed, of the money he spent, of the amount he owed each of his friends, which he always repaid, "maybe 30 years too late."

Once, without a centime to his name, he exchanged pages of one of his manuscripts for "a good lay." When he was without funds, he would go to a cafe—Le Select, La Rotunde, or Le Dome—and order beverages and food and sit there, with the plates, cups, and saucers stacked up beside him, until someone he knew came along, sat down, enjoyed his company, and offered to pay the bill. He was a marvelous conversationalist, an enrapturing storyteller. His French was so hilarious—a combination of street argot spoken by pimps and prostitutes, the medieval French of his reading, and misused subjunctive verbs, all spoken with a heavy New York accent—that his friends were happy to pay for the pleasure of his company.

Within a month of his arrival, Miller had infiltrated the expatriate community in Paris by hanging out on the *terrasses* of Montparnasse cafes, and life became much easier. When he ran into Alfred Perlès at a cafe in April 1930, his fortunes changed, for Perlès became his "guardian angel" and "bosom companion." Miller was impressed by the way Perlès lived his life according to the motto "Easy does it." After Miller's tempestuous life with June, this was a welcome change. Perlès paid off Miller's debts, introduced him to other expatriates, read his work in progress, offered him a place to stay, got him a job as proofreader for the Paris edition of the *Chicago Tribune*, and most important, treated him as a writer to be reckoned with. In the early days of their friendship, before Perlès left for work, he would "leave money on the mantelpiece" for Miller's breakfast.

The two set up house together in Clichy, a suburb of Paris, in a flat with a kitchen and two bedrooms, with bedbugs crawling on the walls. Miller described it as "a happy period." When they ate at home, Miller cooked; his favorite recipe was a stew. He and Perlès led a disciplined life. Both worked as proofreaders for the *Tribune* during the night, awakened at noon, took a meal together. Miller wrote, went bike riding, and explored Paris in the afternoons. Before they went to their office, they ate their supper at a workingman's restaurant, then worked from eight P.M. to two A.M.

Miller's first writing in Paris was about the city and his daily life there. In his notebooks, he recorded his impressions of what he saw, what he heard, what he experienced, as he studied the city. He wrote about pissoirs, flea markets, Kandinsky, surrealism, abbatoirs, the Grand Guignol, the lesbians at the Jockey Club, the fairgrounds at rue de Lapp. He sent encyclopedic letters to his friend Emil Schnellock in New York describing each of his days: "what happened to me—what I discovered about Paris." These notes and letters became the foundation for his Paris sketches, and later, *Tropic of Cancer*.

The life Miller chose to live in Paris—unattached to material circumstances, senseless acquisition, and "busy bee activity"— permitted him to become a writer dedicated to the process of literary creation, without regard for its financial rewards: "It's not what I have written," he said, "it's the writing itself."

According to Perlès, Miller at work was a spectacle to behold. He could knock out fifteen to twenty pages in a work session. Miller would be hunched over his typewriter (a gift from his lover Anaïs Nin), a Gauloise bleue bummed off Perlès clenched between his teeth, his head encircled by smoke, his fingers flying over the keyboard in the fastest typing Perlès ever witnessed. At times, colored pencils in hand, he stopped to hunt for a passage in one of the piles of books gathered around him or in his Paris notebooks. He would consult one of the letters he sent documenting his days (he almost always kept copies); refer to one of the complicated charts that he pinned up over his work area; check the list of words he'd garnered from his dictionary that he wanted to include in his novel.

He could work, Perlès said, even with others present, even while carrying on conversations with them, sometimes transcribing them into his work even as they were taking place. At times, he would put on a record while writing or burst into song himself. His work, Perlès said, was done while singing. After a writing session, Miller would take his notebook and go on long walks to find new material. Or he would take a bicycle ride to clear his head and observe parts of Paris he hadn't yet visited.

When Miller moved out of Clichy, it was into an apartment at 18 Villa Seurat. His second stay there was in 1934 with his lover Anaïs Nin. The street was famous as a residence of painters, sculptors, writers, and musicians. For the first time, Miller lived in comfort. His relationship with June had ended; during a visit to Paris to see him in 1934, she scribbled a note on a bank statement, "get a divorce as soon as possible," ending their "tempestuous and unbelievably romantic" ten-year relationship.

While living at Villa Seurat, Miller wrote *Black Spring*, began and abandoned a tome on D. H. Lawrence that completely obsessed him, began and completed two revisions of *Tropic of Cancer*, wrote *Tropic of Capricorn*, and composed several short works. For the book on Lawrence, Miller read all of Lawrence's work and made complex charts of Lawrence's ideas and the interrelationships among them. The work came to eight hundred pages before Miller discovered he was "so mixed up" that he "started contradicting himself." He decided to abandon the book, the only one he never finished.

Free of this burdensome project, Miller began *Tropic of Cancer*, about what it takes for a working-class man, without benefit of a college education or family money or financial support of any kind, to become a writer and what he must go through to live a creative life. "How the hell can a man write when he doesn't know where he's going to sit the next half-hour," says the narrator of *Cancer.* "One can sleep anywhere but one must have a place to work. . . . Even a bad novel requires a chair to sit on and a bit of privacy." *Cancer* is about Miller's "down and out" life in Paris as an aspiring writer, his sexual adventures in Paris, his theories about fiction, and his relationship with June, in which he cast himself as "a desperado of love."

At the Villa Seurat, Miller began the mature phase of his writing life. Nin insisted that he write *Tropic of Cancer* in his own voice, the "first person spectacular": "Out with the balderdash, out with the slush and drivel, out with the apostrophes, the mythologic mythies, the sly innuendoes, the vast and pompous learning. . . . Out—out damned fly-spots. . . . What I must do . . . is to write a few simple confessions in plain Milleresque language. No flapdoodle. . . . No entomological inquests, no moonlight and flowers." Years later, he remarked, "I found my voice in Paris."

Miller had promised June he would write a novel about her, and he kept that promise. But the shape of his intended novel changed drastically. Because of Nin, he was more secure; she persuaded him to set forth "a new cosmogony of literature." Rather than centering the work on June, Miller now made himself the heart and soul of the work. June's story was still there, but it was just one of many anecdotes about Miller's life, albeit an important one. The novel became an autobiographical work that was a catchall for Miller's experiences in Paris, his love of June and her betrayal, his thoughts about what he read, his theories about the novel, his answer to James Joyce's Dublin experiences in *Portrait of the Artist as a Young Man*, for it described how Miller effected his transformation from a love-besotted loser into a working-class writer.

The most important love affair in the novel was now Miller's love affair with Paris. Not the Paris of the guidebooks, but the Paris he experienced during his first two years there. *His Paris.* The Paris of bums, pimps, prostitutes, "down and outers," philosophers, voracious readers, poor aspiring writers. The Paris that had prompted him to live his life in a new way and that had made him into a writer.

In 1932, his friend Emil Schnellock wrote Miller, asking him if he would ever come back to the United States. Miller responded that "nothing but catastrophe" would make him return. Although he knew he would never become a European, he knew too that he would "never become an American." He had become "an expatriate, a voluntary exile," a man with "no country, . . . and no army to fight for." He now felt like "all the great vagabond artists must have felt: absolutely reckless, childish, irresponsible, unscrupulous, and overflowing with carnal vitality, vigor, ginger, etc. Always on the border of insanity due to worry, hunger, etc. But shoving along day after day."

Once, when Miller was asked to describe his ideal day, he remarked he could never have lived such a day unless he'd rejected the idea of living in luxury. From when he moved to Paris with just ten dollars in his pocket, he'd learned that the only way for him to be free enough to live life on his own terms was to eschew possessions and to follow his instinct to move.

"All my life," he wrote, "it seems I have never chosen the

place to live. I've just been put there, by force of circumstance." He remarked that he never chose to move to Paris, that he was impelled there because he couldn't live a writer's life in the United States; that he never chose to move to Greece, that he would have preferred staying in France, but that he was forced to leave in 1939 because of the war; that he never chose to leave Greece and return to the United States, but that the American consul took his passport and ordered him to return to New York; that he never chose to live in Big Sur, California, but that he just found himself there.

But wherever he moved, "a totally new world" opened and he found himself having experiences he'd never dreamed of before and changing in ways he'd never imagined, becoming someone far different from the man he'd been. In Paris, he became a writer. In Greece, he learned about "the world of nature and of sacred places." In Big Sur, "another sublime place," he discovered a "loneliness" that was "marvelous" for him. There, he never had any trouble writing because there were so few distractions. "I wrote every day, always from a fresh source," he said. It was such an important haven that Miller advised anyone coming to see him to "check your neuroses and psychoses at the gate."

Moving from one place to another was essential, Miller believed, for a transformation of the self, which could occur only if you were open to what the new place offered and if you shed your old self like a snake's skin. "When I look back at myself," he said, "I don't see *a* self. I see many selves." Whenever Miller moved away from a place—save for his return to France—he never moved back, because he no longer was the man he'd been. "Once I leave a place," he said, "I leave it for good."

Many people, Miller believed, were terrified by change. They protected themselves from it by doing each day what they didn't want to do to earn money to buy what they didn't need. This, he believed, was a form of suicide. "It would be better if a man did what he liked to do and failed than to become a successful nobody."

Miller thought the world would be a better place if people were taught not to care about possessions; instead, they should be taught to become "idlers, enjoy, relax, not care, not worry." He had transformed himself into that kind of man, one willing to continually evolve, and he had created a life for himself that made it possible.

In his older age, when he was living in California, he described his ideal day. It would be a day revolving around "being" rather than "doing." It would be "a day to myself. . . . I would get up very late; only when I felt like jumping out of bed with vigor and vim. I would have no regard for time." After a good swim, he would meet a friend, play Ping Pong. At night, he would have a French meal ("No health food" was a motto) and watch a good movie. "Finally," he said, "I'd read. I always read in bed and I always have about six or eight books at the bedside."

In 1934, *Topic of Cancer* was published in Paris in a small edition while Miller was living at the Villa Seurat. But because of obscenity laws, it wasn't published in the United States until 1961, nearly thirty years after it was written. By then, Miller was sixty-nine years old and living in Pacific Palisades, California; he'd waited a long time for his work to be recognized in the United States. The U.S. edition of *Cancer* was published by Grove Press, which had won a landmark case brought against D. H. Lawrence's *Lady Chatterley's Lover.* This victory liberalized obscenity laws; thereafter any socially significant work—and *Cancer* was deemed such a work—was guaranteed constitutional protection regardless of its content.

In 1961, Henry Miller visited Paris, returning to the places he'd lived, the sites he'd loved, the cafes he'd frequented. On his way back to California, he stopped in New York to see June once more. She was, he said, living in a miserable dump on Clinton Avenue in Brooklyn.

June was no longer the mythic character, the ravishingly beautiful woman he'd last seen in Paris and celebrated in his work. She had become a frail, crippled, toothless, nearly blind old woman, although she still seemed courageous and charismatic. In comparison with her, Miller felt he had aged wonderfully well. He believed himself to still be "rakish, handsome, dapper, full of energy and exhilaration." *Tropic of Cancer* had been the block-buster of the year and he was now famous, though not yet rich from the novel's sales, something he never cared about.

Disturbed by the vision of what June had become, Miller wanted to leave her apartment quickly. But June expected him to stay longer, even tried to seduce him. Miller understood, as he never had before, that if he hadn't moved to Paris when he did without her, he too would have wound up like this—old, poor, sick, alone. And with his dream of becoming a writer unrealized.

EIGHT

Moving On

MOVING'S ANCIENT HISTORY . . .

Human beings, as we now know, have been constantly on the move since soon after our species emerged in sub-Saharan Africa. Uncountable scores of our ancestors—except for the African Bush people, who still live in the Kalahari Desert where human life originated—have moved.

My mitochondrial DNA indicates that an ancient fore-mother of mine (no doubt with a small group of others) walked west out of the Kalahari Desert many thousands of years ago. About eighty thousand years ago, her descendants (my ancestors), moved northeast in stages, most likely following "a newly emerging corridor of grassland" during the African Ice Age. All these moves were accomplished by walking: "As a species, we colonized the world on foot," Rory Stewart, author of *The Places in Between*, has said.

In stages, her descendants (my ancestors) moved farther north, across the Sinai Peninsula (present-day Egypt). Finding the desert harsh, they moved, in stages, into the eastern Mediterranean and western Asia roughly sixty thousand years ago.

My female ancestors spent several thousand years in the Near East, until one or more of them moved west across Anatolia (present-day Turkey), then north across the Caucasus Mountains of Georgia and southern Russia, establishing, and then leaving, one settlement after another with other tribal members all along this route.

In time, her descendants moved into the Rhine River Basin, where historical records indicate Ashkenazi Jewry was founded. At some point—and here the story is clouded and cannot be traced—one of her descendants (one of my ancestors) moved south, perhaps in stages, settling at some point in one of the farthest reaches of what is now modern-day Italy, in a village in Puglia on the tip of the Gargano Peninsula facing the Adriatic.

At some point, either late in the nineteenth century or very early in the twentieth, my birth grandmother left Puglia, traveling to a port by foot or donkey cart, boarded a ship, and migrated to the United States, where she married my grandfather, who had traveled to the United States from the same place, undertaking the same journey. My grandfather had lived an itinerant life working on the railroad before they married, settled in Hoboken, New Jersey, and lived together for a short time, during which my grandmother gave birth to my mother; my grandmother died during the influenza epidemic that killed so much of the world's population.

Like most of us, I come from a people on the move, and knowing my ancestors have been on the move for many thousands of years puts my own moves into perspective. My move to Montclair was a fortunate move, a chosen one. But most of my ancestors' moves, until my parents' and my generation, so far as the record suggests, seem to have been caused by climate change (in my grandparents' case, a severe drought in the South of Italy), by populations in settlements reaching critical levels, or by cataclysmic natural or historical events. Although the reasons for my moves do not parallel theirs, still, the very act of moving connects me to my ancient and more recent ancestors, and the meaning of their moves imbues the meaning of mine.

MY GRANDFATHER'S MOVE TO AMERICA . . .

As my father told me the history of how my Southern Italian grandfather came to the United States to work on the railroad and eventually settle in Hoboken, I wondered why he had left Italy, wondered what to call him. Was he an immigrant, an emigrant, an émigré, or a refugee? Settling this mattered to me, because I believed that his history was embedded in my own. My birth grandmother's history, my father said, was sketchy—all he knew about her was that she came from the same part of Puglia as my grandfather. My stepgrandmother left a village in Puglia during World War I; she was a "mail-order bride" my grandfather sent for to help him raise my mother. Conditions in Italy were brutal during the war, and many men had been killed; my stepgrandmother was grateful to leave, no matter what the circumstances. She grew to love my grandfather, though their relationship was "testy," as my father put it; my mother, however, she felt no affection for.

My grandfather's story is the most complete. As a young man, he left the South of Italy, where he was a farmworker during the era of the great migration. Because he had never before left his village, he could not predict the immensity of his journey, the distance he would travel, the time it would take by walking, donkey cart, or railroad to his port of embarkation. Nor could he imagine the size of the ship he'd board to take him to that foreign land he'd heard about only in story, the breadth of the ocean he'd cross, the discomfort of the journey, the travails when he arrived, the difficulties on entering the United States, the difference between the ancient place he'd left and the modern world he'd arrive in. The only way I've come to understand something of what this journey entailed was by viewing Emanuele Crialese's epic film *Nuovomondo* (The Golden Door), about a family's emigration from Sicily; the only way I've come to understand something of what my grandfather endured in Puglia was in hearing my father's stories of my grandfather's life, recalling my grandparents' stories, and reading Frank M. Snowden's *Violence and the Great Estates in the South of Italy: Apulia, 1900–1922*.

Family legend has it that the day my grandfather left home, his mother helped him pack everything he would take into a very large headscarf, tying the corners together to form a cumbersome bundle. A few changes of long underwear, a few shirts. Birth, communion, and confirmation certificates, passport and transit documents. Some dry biscuits to eat on the journey.

There were no photographs of his parents. Over the years, my grandfather forgot their faces. When my mother grew into girlhood, he wept, for his child brought the image of his mother's face back to him, and for this he was both glad and sorry.

Like so many others, after his long journey my grandfather found himself alone in a country whose language and mores he did not know and would never understand. Everyone he loved, everything he knew, had vanished. Unlike those who came to make money and planned to return, my grandfather could not retrace his journey. He was, we believe, an anarchist who had agitated for social change, hoping landowners would make concessions to workers for more pay and better working conditions. He even hoped his descendants might receive an education. He was like many others who protested the stranglehold the rich had on the poor, the starvation wages paid to farmworkers (often working on land once held in common but confiscated from the poor with the collusion of government and church), the extortionist prices the landowners demanded for rent and food, the dehumanizing customs (the interdiction against farmworkers joining landowners during the *passeggiata*, the ritual evening walk; the refusal of landowners to sit down at the same table with farmworkers to discuss their demands; the right of landowners to deflower the bride of a farmworker on her wedding night).

Whether my grandfather left Italy because he participated in the frequent, bloody strikes in the south and was a wanted man, I can't say. But there seemed a necessary silence surrounding his departure. He said he came to the United States for a better life. But when I asked my father why my grandfather came, he said, "He came, really, because he was afraid."

Puglia, the province my grandfather left, was called the "land of massacres." When he fled, there were forty-five strikes involving 109,000 workers, one of whom I suspect was my grandfather. And so I believe it was not really fear but terror that propelled him across the ocean. In the year he left, farmworkers were murdered by hired thugs for supporting strikes, foraging for food on private property, acting insubordinately to overseers, violating curfew, supporting political candidates who favored unionizing farmworkers, discussing unionizing farmworkers, being anarchists, or being affiliated with anarchists.

My grandfather waited nearly forty years to become a naturalized citizen of the United States, applying soon after the United States and Italy became allies later in the war. I don't know why it took him this long to sever ties with his homeland. Perhaps it was his distrust of government. Perhaps he harbored secret dreams of moving back to Italy.

Still, my grandfather's Hoboken neighborhood became his village. He lived there until he died, could not imagine moving to the suburbs where no one spoke his dialect. Hoboken became a comforting, familiar space. It recalled the crowded-together village of his childhood. He liked walking to the saloon around the block to talk politics; sitting on a folding chair on the sidewalk in summer to watch his neighbors walk by; playing pinochle by the light of the streetlamp with his cronies on the card table they'd set up outside on hot summer nights; helping his daughter shop at Fiore's across the street for Italian delicacies he could never have afforded in Italy; gardening on his fire escape; leaning out his kitchen window with a slingshot to kill pigeons, which he would fry on his coal stove; making wine in the basement. These small pleasures mattered, made life meaningful.

I sometimes wonder if my grandfather was truly happy in Hoboken. If he ever felt safe there. If he had come to the point in his life where he thought that a serene, secure life was possible.

AMBIGUOUS LOSSES . . .

The writer Pauline Boss has described how so many people in the United States feel a sense of loss when they move, deeper, even, than the experience seems to warrant. In *Ambiguous Loss*, she describes growing up in an émigré community in the Midwest where everyone came from abroad in search of a better life. To come here, émigrés severed ties with their homeland and families, causing a tremendous sense of loss, which in many families was never discussed, although its effects were felt. "Homesickness," says Boss, "became a central part of my family's culture"; because of this, she felt she didn't know "where home really was." Even with the passage of time, that profound sense of separation never ebbed for her, never was resolved. Grief at having moved and living in exile was an unspoken substratum of her family's existence. Still, Boss lived with the consequences of her family's sorrow; their story affected her even though she didn't know it.

As an adult, when Boss moved, she—like I—felt a profound sense of loss even though she knew she was moving to a better environment with more opportunities for her. She couldn't view the new place as home because she'd learned that every move breeds a sense of dislocation. It took much reflection and soul-searching for her to understand that a child from a family like hers can act as if moving necessarily entails grief that will never dissipate. "Unless people resolve . . . the incomplete or uncertain loss . . . that is inherent in uprooting," she writes, "the legacy of frozen grief" may affect them and their families for years.

THE PATTERN OF MY MOVES . . .

As I read about the moves made by people I've written about in these pages, I learned that each developed a story about their life-long moving history—why they moved, how their lives were affected, how they grew as people, what their homes came to mean to them. They discovered a pattern to their moves, often originating in childhood, allowing them to understand important aspects of why they moved and how their moves affected them. This, many people—including myself until recently—rarely do. But reflecting on our moves allows us to understand something profound and necessary about ourselves.

The creative people described in these pages developed a mythology about their lives and how their moves contributed to changes in their lives and work. Henry Miller, realizing his move to Paris enabled him to put the difficult and torturous past behind him, live for the moment, and become the "Proust of Brooklyn," the esteemed writer he'd never have become had he stayed in the United States. Eavan Boland, understanding her move to the suburbs threatened to turn her, as a suburban matron, into the ironic subject of someone else's poetry unless she shifted the aesthetic of her work to celebrate that life. Virginia Woolf, knowing that during middle age she needed the excitement of living in London to break new ground as an experimental writer. Vita Sackville-West, realizing she wanted a house connected to her family's history because she couldn't inherit her ancestral home. Eugene O'Neill, learning that because of his nomadic childhood, he never felt at home anywhere. D. H. Lawrence, knowing he was embarking on a relentless, unrealizable quest for a domestic Eden, but continuing nonetheless. Elizabeth Bishop, accepting that although she believed she'd searched for an ideal home, she'd really wanted a transcendent love. Sigmund Freud, understanding he needed his archaeological collection with him, for it helped him feel rooted, helped him conceptualize his theories, especially in exile. Pierre Bonnard, learning how his move to the south of France utterly changed his art and how close attention to one beloved home could be inspiriting. Carl Jung, following his intuitive compunction to build, allowing the process to help him plumb the common needs of human beings. Mark Doty, learning that he needed community at one stage, and later, solitude to shift the imagistic ballast of his poetry.

These creative people elevated the act of moving in their lives from the merely humdrum to one of the most significant acts they—or any human being—would undertake. Their reflections attest to the fact that where we live matters deeply, that where we move to can enrich our lives, that wrong moves can be harmful, and that forced moves can prove tragic. If we, like they, become conscious about why we want to move, and understand what we need rather than what we want, our moves will satisfy us deeply. If we don't, the results can be harmful, as Shelley's life demonstrates. Attesting to the profound impact of moving on our lives, these creative people urge us to consider the complex subtext of moving's meanings.

Before I wrote this book, if anyone had asked me why I'd moved from one place to another, I couldn't have answered. I would have said that I hadn't moved very much at all, though, in fact, my moving history is close to the national average—though I spent more time in Teaneck than most people spend in one place. I would have said that I don't like to stir things up in my life, that I don't like the unknown, that I like stability—and to some extent this is true, although I didn't know why. I would have said that every move I'd made in adulthood I hadn't initiated or chosen. When pressed, I would have admitted that I did move primarily to get rid of something in a place that had made it less desirable over time. I would never have said that any of my moves replicated the patterns of those of my ancestors, nor that I was impelled to move because of historical circumstances. I had no idea of the pattern behind my moves until I thought about them in the ways my subjects had.

The first move: Fourteenth Street, Hoboken, to Fourth and Adams, Hoboken, New Jersey. My grandparents move my mother and me from a tenement on Fourteenth Street near the docks into a tenement on Fourth and Adams in a mostly Italian neighborhood— the apartment is next door to my maternal grandparents'—while she and I are staying with relatives. I am an infant; it is during World War II and my father is in the Pacific. The move is precipitated by an incident profoundly affecting my mother, making my grandparents realize my mother and I aren't safe on Fourteenth Street. My father learns, by letter, the barest outline of the story.

Our apartment is invaded by rowdy sailors, on leave from a ship docked at the piers. They've mistaken our apartment for a whorehouse. My mother takes me away to visit relatives. While we're away, my grandparents move our belongings. We move because my mother has been terrorized in her own home: there is a war, my father is not home to protect my mother, my parents have been forced to live in a dangerous neighborhood near the docks because of a housing shortage when they married.

Because of this move, I learn a move can enrich a life, and I gain many benefits. Life within an extended family—I usually spend time with someone wanting to be with me. A love of physical activity—I can play in a nearby park and participate in roller skating and playing ball, which had been impossible on the sidewalk of Fourteenth Street. A love of reading—we're too poor to buy books, but we're now near a library we can visit frequently. A passion for Italian food—our neighborhood is filled with food stores and pastry shops. An understanding of the importance of friendship—here my mother meets women vital to her well-being during and after the war. A sense of safety—my grandparents live next door. A sense of the importance of community—our apartment building, during the war, has an "open door" policy, and we kids migrate from one apartment to another, and our mothers gather for coffee and tea during the day.

But the move itself is unsettling. I learn that a home might not be a safe place, though I also learn that it's important to move from such a place. We live in one place, we go away, we return to another, and nothing is said about why. I lose a sense that I'm the most important person in my mother's life, not an altogether bad thing, and lose the serenity of our former household, for once we move, my mother and her stepmother (my grandfather's second wife) fight whenever my grandfather isn't around to broker a peace.

The second move: Fourth and Adams in Hoboken to Prospect Avenue in Ridgefield, New Jersey. My father is home from the war; I'm seven years old, my sister, born after the war, is three. My grandfather has died and my parents move into a house in the suburbs, my stepgrandmother coming with us. I live here until I go away to college, though I return summers and holidays. I finally move out when I marry at twenty-one (and none too soon, I tell myself).

When my father is very old, he tells me that it is the dream of owning such a house that helps my mother keep her spirits up during the war; this dream helps him too. They wrote to each other, he tells me, of the life they would lead in that imagined house, the family all together, a proper kitchen, a proper bathroom with a tub and shower, a bit of lawn, a garden, enough bedrooms so they don't have to share a room with their offspring, as they do in Hoboken.

Before the war, my father's desires are few: a car, a yearly road trip, a motion picture camera, peace and quiet at the end of a day's work. Before he goes away, my father believes he'll live in Hoboken for the rest of his life: only the well-to-do own homes, so he's never indulged himself in this impossible dream because he's learned it's best not to want what you can't have. But after the war, veterans can buy houses because they can secure mortgages.

During the war, my mother reads *Ladies' Home Journal*

articles about the dream homes that will be built for returning members of the armed forces and their families after the war—ranch houses, split levels, houses you could build from kits—and she shows me pictures of those houses. My mother never wanted a new house; she wanted an old house with period details, a "fixer-upper" that she and my father could restore. My mother always admired fine things; she wanted a house with wood moldings and floors, generously proportioned rooms, large windows. But the only way she thought she could get one was if the house was derelict. I think too she wanted a house she could rescue so she and my father could turn chaos into order and ugliness into beauty, for doing this was immensely satisfying to them both. They liked to work hard, to create something together.

They find their dream house in 1949 in Ridgefield, a small suburban community with neat houses set back from tree-lined streets on small plots of land with lawns, shrubs, and gardens, ten miles north of Hoboken, a world away. The house is an old Victorian, on a small rise on a corner lot at the apex of one of Ridgefield's two hills. On the other hill, mostly undeveloped woodland and higher in elevation, is the former site of an important art colony that had included Man Ray; one of his paintings of Ridgefield, *The Hill*, depicts our house.

The house looks like a wreck the first time my parents see it—buckling wallpaper, worn wooden floors, and a tiny, dark, ancient kitchen. It feels unwanted, unloved, and forlorn, and it needs rewiring and new plumbing, but my father knows he can learn how to make the house livable. It has amenities that the Hoboken tenement lacks: central heating; hot water; a proper eat-in kitchen with a gas stove and oven and an electric refrigerator; a dining room; a bathroom with a toilet, tub, and shower; three bedrooms (one with a sleeping porch); a big basement where my father can build a workbench. My parents can see how, with hard work—stripping wallpaper, sanding floors—they can make it beautiful. Perhaps they think that this work will bring them together, as decorating their first apartment has, and undo the adverse effects of the war. My father wants to believe that they can recapture the wonderment of creating a home together.

But men like my father who come home from war can't leave their war experiences behind on the curb to be tossed away as so much garbage. The men they become move into new homes promising so much but not delivering that one thing they crave: a life that will erase the war, that can recover the men they've left behind.

My father knows he'll work hard to improve this place, and I suspect this is just what he needs to tamp down his memories— he'd witnessed thousands of men dying when a munitions boat explodes, seen pilots dying when their aircraft overshot a runway. My mother hopes the move will change my father back into the man he was before the war, for he comes home moody, irritable, prone to rages; she hopes everything will fall into place and they'll be as happy as they should be during peacetime.

Moving to Ridgefield, I gain a love of nature from our walks through the wooded parts of town (soon to be lost to development) and visits to the wetlands (soon lost to the New Jersey Turnpike). A freedom to play in the street, riding bikes, jumping rope, and playing tag. More privacy, for my sister and I share a room apart from my parents, though for reasons of economy, my parents bought only one bed for us, so this is a compromised privacy. A desire to continue my education, which in Hoboken would have been difficult; Ridgefield's schools were better. A love of crafts, developed in summer camps run by the town. A passion for knitting, learned from my grandmother. An ability to earn money because of jobs available for young people.

But I lose a vibrant street life, for—except for children playing—the streets of Ridgefield are quiet, and grown-ups don't gather outside. I lose my independence, too, for in Ridgefield I have to watch my sister most of the time.

I understand now that the strain on my parents after the move must have been considerable. My father has a long commute, a long workday, he comes home exhausted, then works on the house; my mother has child care, ordinary household tasks, plus major projects—sewing curtains, removing weeds and dead bushes, scraping wallpaper. But she suffers the loss of her friends and the communal life Hoboken provides, for there are no public gathering places for women in this town, no opportunities for my mother to engage in casual conversation. She is cooped up all day because she doesn't drive and hasn't yet made friends. Even buying groceries is difficult: the only shop in town is a very long walk down and then up a steep hill—hard to manage while carrying heavy parcels.

But there are good times too. My mother creates a rock garden on the side of our house that people in the neighborhood greatly admire, eventually makes fast friends, enjoys spending time on our back porch. She continues to engage in her creative projects—sewing clothes, making curtains, baking. My father joins the local volunteer fire department—men, many of them veterans, who formed a congenial and supportive group for him. Eventually, he becomes chief, putting the leadership he's learned during war to peacetime use. He takes up stained-glass making, reads historical accounts of his war, listens to opera, builds models of historic aircraft carriers, like the ones he's served on.

The third move: Prospect Avenue in Ridgefield to Summit Avenue in Jersey City, New Jersey. I am twenty-one, newly married, and my husband and I move into an affordable apartment in a gritty neighborhood near where he goes to medical school. I'm teaching in a school half an hour away, but we reason his hours will be longer than mine, so I should commute.

I wanted to leave home as soon as possible after college. But during the sixties, it was rare for a young woman to establish her own home without marrying. Since I'd fallen in love, I wanted to marry sooner than later. But I was desperate also to escape my parents' household, because my parents had become deeply critical of me.

In October 1962, the Cuban Missile Crisis occurs. For fourteen days, the United States and the world live poised on the verge of nuclear war. My future husband and I spend a weekend together during that agonizing time. I remember nothing about it, except how we clutch at one another, believing we could be killed at any moment, living as close as we do to New York City. We vow if we survive—and we are nearly certain we won't—we will marry as soon as we can afford to, and that we'll set up house together. It is one of the turning points in our lives, this brush with annihilation, and when we enter married life and move to our first home, it is with a newfound sense of vulnerability. (There is something of a congruence here between my grandfather's terror propelling him across the ocean to America and mine and my husband's rushing us into a three-room apartment in Jersey City. In fact, each of my moves is remotely connected to feeling my life or well-being was threatened.)

The apartment we move into looks a lot like the one in the Bronx where my husband lived as a boy, and Jersey City reminds me of Hoboken, where I felt so comfortable—its architecture, its gritty charm. We each find reminders of cherished childhoods in this apartment. Where we lived as children has been one of the reasons for our compatibility—we both come "from the old neighborhood."

We'd missed the vitality of small-city life—the press of people on the streets, the opportunities for chance encounters, the coming and going of friends into and out of apartments. Our lives had both changed dramatically, and not altogether for the better, when our families had moved to the suburbs. For although we were ensconced in houses that our parents owned, and we had a lot more room and backyards, our mothers' isolation made itself felt in both our lives. We missed our childhood friends, mourned what we'd lost, but had no name for what we were experiencing—we were told that we were far better off than before.

Moving to Jersey City, I gain a sense of independence; two new women friends; a love of homemaking—decorating (on a shoestring), cooking. We have a solid beginning to our marriage and a wonderful social life with friends with common interests (literature, opera, jazz, art). I lose, though, childhood friends, for Jersey City was—is—hard to get to from Ridgefield, and the kind of tranquility that comes from living in a tree-lined neighborhood.

The fourth move: Summit Avenue in Jersey City to Cranford, New Jersey, forty miles from our families, twenty miles from our closest friends. My husband is now an intern; I'm twenty-five and pregnant. I've stopped teaching—mandated in those days for pregnant women—to begin a family. We relocate to an apartment in a two-family house because we believe we should raise our child in the suburbs. Without realizing it, we're recapitulating our parents' moves. We have our first child in November of the year we move there.

I know now that what propels us out of Jersey City is not really a desire to raise a family in the suburbs, but that I become too terrified to continue to live there. We're robbed in the first week in our new apartment. I come home from work and open the door while the robbery is in progress. I run to a neighbor's and call the police, but the robber has fled. We have the locks changed; we have a dead bolt installed. But we live on the first floor, with windows opening onto a courtyard, and I never again feel safe here, even though we stay on for four years. Because the apartment is affordable, we ignore warning signs of the fact that it is in a dangerous neighborhood.

Some time later, prostitutes move upstairs, and the clatter of their clients going up and down the stairs next to our bedroom goes on all night long. We joke about it to our friends, not admitting its adverse impact on our lives. But what finally drives us away is a murder in our building. The victim's body is found near the mailboxes. Immediately after, we decide to move. Not yet knowing what made my mother leave our Fourteenth Street apartment in Hoboken, I don't then understand the similarity between that move and my own, and between my mother's move to suburbia and mine.

What I gain from this move is a temporary sense of safety, soon shattered, for this is where, after the birth of our son, our marriage founders. Here, though, I begin a reading program to help me get through this difficult time, studying self-selected subjects as if I were still in college. I decide never again to live so far from friends and family, for although I'd wanted an independent life, I realize how difficult it is to raise a child without help and support nearby. My parents and I draw closer because, now a parent myself, I realize the difficulty of child rearing. I decide I'll attend graduate school and return to work as soon as I can; I no longer want to depend on someone else for my livelihood, and I miss teaching.

After this move, I almost lose my marriage. My husband has an affair, who knows why, perhaps because I am miserable there, perhaps because of his own personal demons, perhaps because our lives have changed now that we are parents.

This is the worst day I remember. It's early morning after a nighttime blizzard. My husband is working a forty-eight-hour shift at the hospital. There's only one can of formula left; I have no car, not that I could have driven on the icy roads even if I had one; I have no one to call to care for my son. I decide I have to leave my son alone while I walk through the howling wind and driving snow to the nearest store, some distance away. As I walk back home, I realize if anything has happened to my son in my absence, I would be found guilty of negligence. It is the moment I realize we can't live here anymore; we have to get out, and the sooner the better.

The fifth move: Cranford to Palisades Park, New Jersey. We move into an apartment in a two-family house in a working-class neighborhood, ten minutes away from both our parents. My husband is a resident; I am twenty-six, our son is nearly a year old, and, with family nearby, I start graduate school. This is a most fortuitous move. Here, my husband and I repair our marriage. We live in a neighborhood with a strong community that makes life enormously satisfying while I raise our children—our second son is born while we live here.

We find our apartment because of my husband's mother. She knows about the difficulties in our marriage, has had a similar incident in hers, and believes that it is important for a woman in crisis to be near family. She is convinced if we continue to live far away, I will become more depressed and our marriage will end. She volunteers to babysit if we move close so I can attend graduate school and take excursions into Manhattan. She believes we need a "change of scene" to put our crisis behind us, and she is right.

Although my mother-in-law isn't Old World, she believes that mothers need older women around to help them. My generation of women wants independence and a separate life from family. I am smug and self-assured. What I don't count on is that you're never prepared for child rearing, and that staying home all day with a child when you have no friends can be a recipe for disaster.

Still, Palisades Park isn't the easiest place to raise a child. Our apartment is up three steep flights of stairs. Hauling children, baby supplies, carriages, port-a-cribs, laundry, groceries, and garbage up and down the stairs is a rip-roaring pain in the ass. (Here, I understand some small part of how difficult life was for my mother living in a walk-up tenement.)

I discover that I love living close to our parents and they provide an enormous amount of help, without which I could never have earned my degree. I love our working-class neighborhood. It has lots of street life, is within walking distance of food stores and other shops, and close to New York City.

Our babies visit their grandparents often, growing up with them in an almost daily doting attendance. As I clean up one mess or another, I know that I'll soon be dropping my children at their grandparents and that I'll have a blessed few hours to study, shop, or rest. I become a cheerful parent, permitting my children more freedom than friends who don't have this relief, and I certainly reprimand them less.

My marriage becomes far more stable because of where we live. Young parents without family nearby or money enough to hire babysitters (as we couldn't) can't pursue their own desires or further their education as simply as we can. Grateful though I am, I don't realize how much my good fortune, my continuing education, my professional growth, my becoming a scholar and writer, depend on this move my mother-in-law engineers and the subsequent help my family provides.

My husband and I are among the few people on the block who have gone to college, and our neighbors treat us with respect, for we are the professionals they want their children to become. I am welcomed into our neighbors' homes during the day, and they visit mine, but we never socialize at night, a time reserved for family and very close friends. Though we establish firm acquaintanceships, there is an air of impermanence about these relationships, for they know we'll be moving after the end of my husband's residency, and they suspect they'll be staying in this neighborhood for a long time, perhaps the rest of their lives.

I am happy here, happier than in Jersey City or during that calamitous year in Cranford. My origins are working-class and this neighborhood feels comfortable and familiar, drawing me back to when my family lived on Fourth and Adams Street in Hoboken, where kids played sidewalk games and clattered up and down the stairs and into and out of other people's apartments, as they do here in Pal Park, as we call it. It is a neighborhood where if you have to take one of your children to the emergency room, your next-door neighbor will look after your other child. Where people call to ask if you need anything at the supermarket when they run out to shop; where you bake two batches of banana muffins so you can give one away. Where young girls are happy to babysit your kids for a quarter an hour while you cook supper. Where, in summer, ten or more kids crowd into the only above-ground pool on the block while mothers sit around drinking lemonade, taking turns "lifeguarding." Where, if your kids misbehave, you can count on a neighbor to reprimand them. Where people share what they have—a good bottle of wine, a lawn mower, a set of jumper cables, a snow blower, a few folding chairs for company, some stamps, a couple of eggs and a cup of sugar for a cake.

After we live in Pal Park for several years, I miss grass and trees in abundance, and having a bit of open space for my kids to play in—our landlords won't let our kids play in their backyard. I begin to want a view different from that of a smokestack out our living room window. I regret that this working-class neighborhood is not more beautiful, believing, like D. H. Lawrence, that societies should invest money in making working-class neighborhoods as beautiful as those of the well-to-do.

When we live in Pal Park, I often escape with the children to where there is space, fresh air, and trees. We go to Central Park in New York City, to a wading pool in a nearby community, to the banks of the Hudson River, to parkland up Route 9W on the crest of the Palisades, to a children's zoo with a tiny railroad that runs beneath a few minuscule tunnels. Our excursions are taken as much to satisfy me as to please them.

That we are living in a house that isn't ours, that belongs to someone else, begins to be a problem. When we are anyplace but home, I can parent my children the way I choose: I don't inhibit their spontaneous laughter, or tell them not to run so fast, or not to hop up and down; I don't worry that their crying will be greeted with our landlords' raps on the ceiling. Toward the end of our time here, I leave the house for part of each day with the children, going to a park, to a museum, to a food store, to a friend's house, just to get away from the constraints imposed on me by living upstairs from my landlady. This is perhaps why I raise two intrepid sons, boys who become men who love taking trips and excursions, who love adventure. Had we lived in a "dream house" as I raised them, had we stayed put most days, I don't think I would have been inclined to search for exciting places to amuse them. By now I have a good car, enough money for gas. We are counting our pennies, but we are far from destitute.

Another historic event precipitates our move from Palisades Park. We live here during the Vietnam War, which we vehemently oppose. We know that my husband will one day be drafted into the service as a doctor. During his residency, he receives orders to report to Virginia Beach, from where, after training, doctors are sent to Vietnam.

We organize ourselves to move—give up our lease, arrange for movers, bid our friends and family good-bye. I'll live in Virginia Beach until my husband's deployment. Then I'll ponder living on the base or moving back to New Jersey. We are in a state of shock, putting one foot in front of another to get through our days. I believe I am destined to live the life my mother had with a husband away at war like so many other women of my generation.

Just a short time before our move, there is a rollback in the number of troops sent to Vietnam and my husband's orders are rescinded. In the euphoria of that moment, we feel as if we have been spared, and we decide to not postpone anything we can afford that will make our lives more satisfying. We'll look for a new place to live; we'll travel more. My father-in-law, grateful his son is spared, tells us he'll lend us a down payment for a house if we can afford the carrying cost. If we are prudent, we can.

The most important reason to own your own home, if you can afford it, for me is about the simple freedom to live as you desire in your own space. Yes, it is true that if you rent, you don't have to worry about fixing the roof, or mowing the lawn, or repairing leaky faucets. But it also means that you are bound by someone else's rules about how to conduct your life, as we are in this apartment.

The sixth move: Palisades Park to Teaneck, New Jersey. We look for a house in Teaneck, New Jersey, because it is an integrated community, racially, ethnically, and economically diverse. We see an ad for a "charming Tudor-style home, with a beamed cathedral ceiling and stained-glass windows, close to highways and New York transportation." This is important; I am still commuting to graduate school in New York.

We walk in the front door, see the living room, and fall in love. "This is it," my husband says. The room looks like a tiny chapel. I see myself reading in this room, writing in this room, knitting before the fireplace on a wintry night. I think whatever difficulty I have—and there are many, of course, while we live there—sitting in this room, inhabiting it, will ease my pain.

We bid the asking price. Our offer is accepted. We are homeowners for the first time.

So here we are in our thirties, living the American dream of home ownership—my grandfather's dream of owning a piece of America. Kittens, a dog, fish, snakes, hamsters, and a ferret will follow. And we live a very happy life here for more than thirty years, imagining that we'll never again move, although, initially, the loss of the community I've had in Pal Park is difficult, nor have I counted on the hard work of caring for a home.

The seventh move: Teaneck to Montclair, New Jersey. When, years later, we decide to move to Montclair, it is not long after 9/11. One of our sons has witnessed the tragedy; the other loses several friends and acquaintances. We move to be near our grandchildren, yes; but I am moving again in the aftermath of terror—the terror so many of us felt after that day—with the dream that it will dissipate with a change of residence. Leaving the place where I

lived through 9/11, I believe, falsely, will put that experience behind me.

PAL PARK, REVISITED . . .

In the last years of my father's life, when I would visit him in
Ridgefield, I traveled through Pal Park and would see groups of
men standing on street corners. I learned that they are Mayan
people from Guatemala, and they came to Bergen County—some
of them walking all the way—to earn money to send home to
their wives, mothers, and sisters in their villages back home.

They have a dream, like my grandparents did, of establishing a toehold in a land where they can earn a living, where they
can carry on a dignified life. Their labor has bettered the living
conditions of their families: the villages they come from now have
electricity, and the women and children eat better and are health-
ier than before their men left to come to the United States.

Life is difficult for them. The men stand, often before dawn,
just as my grandfather stood in the square in Vieste in Puglia a
hundred years or more ago, hoping, as these men do, that someone will hire them. They wait during the heat of summer, the
cold of the winter. They live many men to a room, often paying
exorbitant rents—a hundred dollars a week or more per man.
Often, they have no money for breakfast, and if they do not get
work for the day, they will not eat lunch or supper either. But, still,
they send much of what they earn back home so their families
can live a better life.

These are the men who you see working throughout this part
of New Jersey, shoveling snow, painting houses, mowing lawns,
weeding gardens, roofing houses, improving homes that are so far
beyond their means they cannot even think about owning them.

Still, these are the men many want to send back where they came from.

Several Korean residents have reached out to these men from Guatemala, for they remember how difficult it was for them when they arrived, the racist graffiti—"Koreans go home"—scrawled on a highway overpass and on the windows of Korean-owned shops. Their first contact was tentative, not understood by the men from Guatemala. A Korean woman arrived with hot coffee and bagels early in the morning at one of the corners where the men waited for work. At first the men were suspicious, but they became grateful for this gesture of friendship. Now there are English-language schools, run by the Korean American community, and it is hoped that this will help ease the Guatemalans into the fabric of American life.

I am certain that, like my grandfather and so many others who came to America, these men too hope their labor will permit their children and their children's children to make a better life for themselves, perhaps here in America. One day, maybe, they'll be able to bring their families here, educate their children, and if they live a long life, they will see their children, or their children's children, buy a home like the ones they work on, move into it, and call it home.

Afterword

A FINAL GESTURE OF FAREWELL . . .
Henry Miller left Paris in June 1939 to move to Greece for a year at the invitation of his friend Lawrence Durrell. Just before he departed, Miller realized he needed to mark this important transition with a ceremony. Paris was where he felt, for the first time, that being a writer was worthwhile. It was where he found his voice as a working-class novelist, where he wrote his masterpiece *Tropic of Cancer* in the "first person spectacular," memorializing his move from the United States to Paris and the man he became there.

Miller suspected he might never return to Paris. He knew that in Greece he would immerse himself in nature and Greece's spiritual history. He expected living there to change him. And so he wanted to create a ceremony that would bring closure to his Paris years.

Paris had given him so much. From his earliest days there, when he was homeless, sleeping in cinemas and under bridges, using the bundle of his manuscripts as a pillow, Miller's immersion in Parisian life had helped alleviate the pain of living without his wife, June. Wandering its streets, Miller learned the difference between one arrondisement and another and sought those places he believed were consecrated by writers who'd lived there. He wrote about everything he saw, everything he learned, in a series of notebooks.

Miller used these notebooks for his Paris sketches and the Paris scenes in *Tropic of Cancer*. But apart from the material they provided for his work, they were a record of his emotional, intellectual, and spiritual growth. They showed how Paris made Miller the man into Miller the writer.

And so when he was ready to leave, Miller gathered all his notebooks and reread them. Reviewing his life in Paris was a prelude to saying good-bye to the city that had made him the kind of writer he'd dreamed of becoming. He realized that throughout the Paris years he'd acted "like a reporter at large," writing in his notebooks about everything he saw, everything he read, everything he felt, everything he was writing about and planned to write. He was so conscientious, he said, that "you'd think I was being paid by a big, important newspaper." There were keepsakes, too, pasted onto the pages—"menus from restaurants, theatre programs, everything"; lists of books he'd read and wanted to read; lists of words he wanted to include in his writing; lists of subjects to write about. The notebooks were treasures, a record of his creative life in Paris.

But Miller chose not to take his notebooks to Greece. He decided to let them go. As a final gesture of farewell to his Parisian life, he had them bound and gave them to friends as parting gifts. He knew he was leaving behind a record of an important part of his life—of the man he'd been in Paris, his essential Parisian self. But he believed leaving them behind was necessary as he ventured on to Greece.

He was a man who traveled light. Besides, he knew the notebooks would be safer with friends who had encouraged him to write in his own voice and who valued his work. Once again he would become a vagabond, the persona that had served him well in his early days in Paris, for it separated him from what was worst about his past and taught him how to embrace the present, no matter how difficult. The man he would become in Greece should arrive there unfettered, ready to embark on another of life's great adventures, open to the experience of each new day.

LEAVE-TAKING . . .

The morning after Ernie and I move to the new house, I have to go back to the old one to await a serviceman. It's the morning of the day we're closing on the sale of our old house and the man is coming to repair a faulty fire alarm. The fire chief will come to inspect the alarm at noon, and unless it functions properly, we can't sell the house.

I don't want to go back to the old house. I want to remember it as it was before we left. But I have no choice. I have the morning off; Ernie doesn't. So it isn't until the day after our move that I see our house empty.

I arrive, admire the garden, which has finally matured just as we are leaving. Will the new owners care for it as we have? Will they deadhead the flowers? Prune away the deadwood? Feed the tree out front that seems to be dying? And if they don't, what then? Will they love this garden as I have? Will they enjoy the weeping cherry? Sit and take their lunch outside under the giant oak in the heat of summer? How can my garden, whose plants and trees and rocks have been carefully chosen so it looks like a Zen garden, become someone else's?

I turn the key in the lock in the side door. Try to open it—it sticks as always. But today I don't kick it open, for today the door will be someone else's and I don't want to risk damaging it. I take a deep breath, walk into the kitchen. And I feel as I once did when I walked down into the earth in Mexico, down into a tomb devoid of light and air and life, a forbidding and claustrophobic place, one I ran from, for it was a dead place, and what I wanted was life, life, life.

But here I can't run, can't leave. I have a job to do and I am a woman who does what she must regardless of her feelings. And today my job is to wait for the repairman and to make sure the alarm is fixed.

Uncomfortable as I am, as much as I don't want to be here, still, I yearn to stay. I wonder whether I can call the whole thing off, tell the buyers I've changed my mind, that I really don't want to move, rehire the movers, bring back all our furniture, all our treasures, to this, my one true home, and set it up exactly as before.

But, of course, I cannot.

I haven't yet bid a proper good-bye to this house, I realize, and I must, even though I don't want to. I must mourn the loss of my home even as I celebrate our move and our dream of a new life in a new place. For if I miss this opportunity, there will never be another. I will probably never come back here, and even if I do, it will not be the same, not mine, for it will be transformed. Even now this is not the place it once was. It has taken but a few hours to change it utterly. And though this is still my house—in the sense that my husband and I still own it—it is no longer my home.

I wonder why, although so many people move, there is no

ceremony I know about for this kind of leave-taking, no ritual specially designed for this moment. My good friend Liz once threw a party to say good-bye to the home where she raised her children before moving on to an independent life in New York City and Paris. But I need a more private leave-taking and so must create my own parting ritual in these last few moments. After all the years we've been together, I owe the house this much: to bid it farewell.

I start to say good-bye on the second floor in my son Jason's room. And the empty room fills with the sound of Jason's voice as a little boy of five soon after we move into this house, sitting on his bed, arranging his baseball cards, naming players as he sorts them into piles, happy that he no longer has to share a room with his noisy and irritating baby brother. I see him as a young man packing up the contents of this room to take to college; see him leaving it to marry; see him helping my husband turn it into an office when our family begins a new business in our home.

I move across the hall to my son Justin's room and smile. For there was always something unusual going on in this room—a boy looking for a snake that had escaped its cage or for a ferret that had somehow burrowed into the insulation in the back of the closet or jumped out the window; a young man trying to mop up the mess a leaking waterbed made, or trying to quiet the far too many friends who crowded themselves into this tiny room; a brave young man venturing farther than any of us had to college; a graduate deciding to move into an apartment of his own.

Between the bedrooms is the bathroom that was always more menagerie than a place for washing and showering, which my sons never seemed to do until they discovered girls. Here lived schoolhouse pets who needed boarding for the summer—mice, gerbils, species of fish I didn't recognize. Somehow, and no thanks

to our haphazard attentions, they managed to live until we returned them (I, with relief) to their proper classroom homes.
Here Jason's monstrously ugly goldfish with protruding eyes,
called Gloobie, lived in a fishbowl too small for it and survived for
years despite our neglect and mismanagement of his (or perhaps
her) ecosystem. When Gloobie died, Jason keened for days and
insisted on a solemn funeral, with homemade coffin, a tattoo
played on a tin can, a family procession to the backyard, and a
rock tombstone to mark the final resting place.

I come to the tiny study—a hallway, really—where I wrote
for many years, just outside these rooms. I worked there because I
wanted to be near the children, ready to tend to them as they
played or through illnesses or after their awakenings from night-
mares while I snatched moments at my desk for my work, then
minutes, then hours. I kept my study there beyond when I should
have, trying to do my work against the cacophony of my sons'
music as one played the bass and the other the drums, or as each
listened to his favorite band played full blast. But the truth is I
wanted to be there, near them, near all that energy, all that ac-
tion, a necessary counterpoint to my writing life.

In the study, a tiny window overlooks the living room, and
another, just beyond where my desk used to be, looks west out at
the trees, and I remember one glorious autumn afternoon, the
trees all gold and rust, when both my children were outside playing and I sat at my desk reading the work of Henry Miller and
glanced up and looked outside at the setting sun, knowing in the
bliss of that moment that I was exactly where I wanted to be, doing what I wanted to do. I told myself, *I'll never leave this house.*

I head down the stairs, the stairs down which my children
never walked but always clattered, Justin so quickly that Ernie
and I were sure one day he'd fall to the bottom and crack his

skull. And when we had a dog and cats, the ruckus would be un-nerving, with Justin, friends, dog, and cats racing down the stairs as fast as they could to goodness knows where. Jason never rushed, even at our urging, especially not at our urging, as sure then as now that nothing is to be gained by moving quickly.

Always, when the children were growing, the bottom stairs were littered with objects—loose-leaf notebooks, games, clothing, sneakers—that they were supposed to carry upstairs but never did unless I threatened drastic punishment. "When," I'd ask, "are you guys going to learn to take your stuff upstairs?" "Never," Jason would tease, ruffling my hair, grabbing his sneakers but not his loose-leaf. "You'll be sorry when we're gone, sorry when this place is as neat as you'd like it to be," he'd shout from the top of the stairs.

And the truth is that when they left, I was and I wasn't sorry. Oh, I missed them immeasurably, their affectionate roughhous-ing, their teasing, their boy-growing-into-young-man charm. But I learned to be in this house differently. I liked the house quiet, liked the time I had there alone.

Besides, they never truly left. After college, after they'd moved into their own places, they made sure to live close enough to come for dinner a few times a week, for Sunday gatherings—we are an Italian family, after all. And when they both began the family business, there they were again, back in the house, back in their rooms, now offices, as workingmen who turned the kitchen into the company dining room, and at that time I very much wanted them to leave so I could have my house back.

Downstairs I enter the tiny sunken living room with the cathe-dral ceiling and stained-glass window, the reason we bought this house. Its proportions are perfect, and whenever I spent time there, I felt like I was in a chapel, in a meditative, sacred space. For this room is the soul of the house, the place I'd retreated to when in pain, when troubled, when confused.

This room could comfort; it could cure; it could turn a bad day good, a good day wondrous. In this room, I spent long, silent pleasurable moments replenishing my spirit. Once I spent a whole day in front of a fire quilting, leafing through some books, quilting some more, dozing, awakening to the sound of rain on the roof, watching the sky turn pink, then baby blue, then navy. I always promised myself more days like that one. The years passed. And though I lingered now and again, it remains the only time I devoted myself to its pleasure for an entire day. How often I have taken it for granted through these years, passed through it with hardly a glance to get the mail, to greet a visitor, to secure a lock, although, when we first moved here, I vowed I would spend a little time here each day. But work, and the daily business of life, got in my way, as these things so often do, and now there is this memory of that one perfect day spent here, and, yes, regret, too, that throughout all those years, there was only this one perfect day.

I go into the kitchen, the heart of the house. Aside from my study, I have spent most of my time in this room, lingering over breakfast, knitting sweaters, piecing quilts, making daily plans, reading cookbooks, organizing meals, eating with my family, or standing at the stove trying out one recipe, then another, then another.

At this table, left behind for the new owners, Ernie read drafts of my works in progress and edited them with respect and kindness. Here my friend Edi and I dreamed up a book and then made it happen, as we sat together through long summer days, drinking cappuccino, eating biscotti, editing essays, marking copy.

In the kitchen, to make time pass—for the repairman is late

for our appointment—I take the worn broom my husband has left behind and begin sweeping. I go upstairs, sweep the bedrooms, the bathroom, my study. I return downstairs, sweep my kitchen (the kitchen, their kitchen), the dining room, living room, front hall, and think how curious it is that I am cleaning for someone else, because although I clean well when I set my mind to it, it is always with great reluctance; I'd much rather be doing something else—making a soup, reading a book, knitting a sweater.

As I sweep, I try to remember that poem of Emily Dickinson's, the one about sweeping up after someone has died, and yes, this sweeping feels like that kind of sweeping. It feels like a special kind of leave-taking, a kind of mourning. I am mourning the home I've lost, hoping I can resurrect its spirit in that other place.

But when will the new house become home? When I've organized its rooms, its closets? When I've hung our paintings, positioned our pottery on top of dressers? When I've cleaned it top to bottom for the first time? Or will it take time? Or will it take not time, but instead a bread baked, a soup made, a journey returned from, an illness survived, a few pages written, a sweater knit, to make the house feel like home?

First, though, I must let this house go. But I can't. Not yet.

I feel like I've betrayed this house, for I'm the one who's leaving. The house can't go anywhere. It certainly can't come with me, though at times I have imagined taking it with me, digging it out of the ground, propping it on stout timbers, and moving it, like the houses I've seen moved from one place to another on the East End of Long Island. How can I think of letting perfect strangers move through its rooms when it's sheltered us so well all these years? How can it go from being mine to being someone else's? And yet if everything about the house can change—the style of its furnishings, the contents of its cabinets and closets, the color of its walls—then why have I loved it so exclusively? While I lived here, I foolishly thought no one else ever would. So now, too, I feel like *I've* been betrayed, even though I'm the one who's leaving.

About leaving this house, I feel sick inside, like a brute, like I've disrespected it, violated it. I feel like I'm abandoning a lover for no good reason. I feel sure the house will miss me, will wish I had stayed on; I feel sure it won't like the new people, for they won't understand it and its special needs and endearing quirks— how it doesn't like curtains on its windows; how it likes its wood-work cared for; how its stained-glass windows must be treated gingerly; how its roof must be cleared of snow.

For this house is not merely a house. It has become imbued with spirit. My spirit, my family's spirit. When I leave today, I'm sure that I'll be leaving something of myself behind, something of myself that will never be found again, something that will remain here.

LIKE GHOSTS IN THE SHADE . . .

Perhaps, though, we never do really leave our old homes. Virginia Woolf, in her short story "Haunted House," describes the spirits of a couple revisiting the house they had once called home. They walk from room to room, looking for a treasure they'd left but can't find—the spirit of the life and joy they'd experienced in this house. They believe their life here still exists in some ghostly other-world within, which they can penetrate. "Here we slept," the woman says. "Kisses without number," her husband adds. To-gether they recall awakening mornings, the sliver of sky glimpsed between trees, the beauty of the garden, how the house felt in summer and during a winter's snow.

The ghosts stop to gaze at the peacefully sleeping people who now live here and wonder whether these residents have experienced as much joy and lightness of heart while living here as they had.

Perhaps like Woolf's ghosts we too haunt the houses we've left. In her diaries, Woolf often spoke of how in memory she still inhabited her old homes—Talland House in St. Ives where she'd summered as a girl, the house at Hyde Park Gate where she'd spent her childhood. The little girl she used to be, the members of her family, she wrote, hung about these places "like ghosts in the shade." For Woolf, the past was never truly over, and at any given moment we could time-travel into the past through memory. So our past life is never past, for we can relive it, oftentimes with a greater intensity than we live our present life: our past always lies, as Woolf said, in "some dim recess of our brains" awaiting our attention.

As a young woman, Woolf revisited St. Ives. Although she couldn't enter Talland House, she got as close to it as she could, hiding behind the escallonia hedge that made its way into *To the Lighthouse*, her novel about that home. She imagined reaching the gate of the house, opening it, and finding herself "among the familiar sights again." Fearing she'd be caught, Woolf contented herself with peering through a chink in the hedge and saw two lighted windows. It appeared, she thought, as if she'd left that very morning.

Musing on the effect of revisiting Talland House, she concluded that seeing where we've once lived can be unnerving, because while it's human nature to want things to stay the same, visiting a former home reminds us that the only constant is change and that we cannot stay the onward rush of time. Still, as Woolf wrote on the eve of her departure from St. Ives, "Something of our own [seems to be] preserved here from which it is painful to part."

TIME TO GO . . .

The repairman comes; he does his work. The fire chief comes; he inspects the alarm. All's well. The house is ready to pass into another family's hands, to begin another life. It's time for me to say good-bye.

When I turn to leave, the house is still, save for dust motes dancing through sunbeams in the downstairs study. Have they danced this way each fine day while I was at my desk trying to wrest words from oblivion, ignorant of what was happening behind me, the simple beauty that could have nourished me, could have given me words had I permitted myself to look up, turn around, and see it?

The refrigerator, satisfied that all is well, turns its compressor off. The sink drips, as it has for years—*plick, plock, plick, plock*—despite all our attempts to fix it. It is this sound more than any other that has marked the passage of my days here, marked the moments I have lived in this house, and it will be the sound I miss most, even though it annoyed me when I lived here.

The house looks forlorn, like it doesn't know what to do with itself right now; it looks like a girl no one has asked to dance, that girl sitting at the edge of twirling couples sipping her soda, putting her cup down on the floor next to her shiny shoes, folding her hands and settling them into her lap, awaiting someone, anyone, to end her lonely despair.

But perhaps the house is not forlorn. Perhaps the house is pausing. Resting (and goodness knows it needs a rest after putting up with a clan like ours for so many years), recovering for a few short days. Gathering the sunlight into itself. Relaxing into the warmth of a beautiful late-summer afternoon. Yielding to an indolence it hasn't known for years. For soon, too soon, it will once again be all business and bustle, all noise and occupation. Perhaps it knows it needs this respite from the chaos it has just endured, the chaos yet to come. All those paintings, photographs, and mirrors torn off its walls. Carpets ripped off its floors. Furniture shoved this way and that. Doors thrown open, then banged shut, without the least concern for common courtesy. And truth be told, this house has seen more than its share of strife and disorder, although not recently, thank goodness. Coffee cups flung at its windows, fists battering its doors, feet kicking its walls. It has heard oaths and imprecations, for the time that we have spent here has not always been serene.

This house—it could tell stories.

But now there is new life promised this house. New narratives will take place within its walls. The woman moving here is pregnant and will give birth to a boy within a few months' time. Soon the house will hear a new baby's cry, smell mother's milk, hear the coo of a father greeting his first offspring, listen to the squeak of a rocking chair as a child lies nestled, nursing, in its mother's arms.

I hope this house will embrace this little family with as much love as it has my own. I wish them as much pleasure from it as I have taken here, but wish them too, less pain. They seem a far more sensible couple than my husband and I were when we moved here, far less prone to histrionics, far more likely to talk things out than shout and stalk away. But here too we learned to modulate our rage, learned to appreciate each other, learned to love well and wisely. A rich life is pain, pleasure, hope, disappointment, longing, fulfillment, love, loss, serenity, agitation, all in full measure.

And life ensures that we will experience some of each, and only the future can tell what the proportion of each shall be for the young couple moving here—for us, for anyone.

Yes, now it's time to go. Time to close the door one last time. Time to let the house, once full of the din of our existence, ease into the loveliness and stillness of its temporary solitude. The house is filled with light and will be after I close and lock the door. But within, a change will take place. It will be empty, but alive with the stillness of expectation.

Some part of the house will settle more comfortably into the ground, and there will be a creak, a groan, that no one will hear. Beyond the house, the hum of the nearby highway will still penetrate, still disturb. Above, airplanes will still dip lower than they ought, roaring their way to the ground a few miles away.

In the next house, on the corner, a woman will check on the progress of her bread dough, place it, fully risen, into her oven, turn on her exhaust fan as it bakes, so the smell of baking bread will waft on the atmosphere to my old house, through the space under the side door, and into the kitchen. Out back, a leaf detaches itself from our neighbor's tree and falls, a prelude to autumn. A bird in flight loses a feather. It drifts to the ground and will lie there later this day as the new owners enter this house to inspect their new home. On the slate patio, the rusted circle made by our children's wading pool, like a Zen enso, remains. No human effort has eradicated it. Someday, perhaps—but not, I think, within my lifetime—rain may pelt the patio clean and erase this mark that we have left behind. But for now the circle remains. Mute testament to the life we lived here.

Acknowledgments

To paraphrase Virginia Woolf, any completed work depends, not exclusively upon the writer, but also upon many others. I wish to thank Geri Thoma, my agent, for guiding me with grace, intelligence, and good humor through nearly twenty years of writing; Julia Galbus, my friend from afar, for daily communications about the creative process and unswerving support; Christina Baker Kline for looking at an early version of the manuscript and discovering just what needed to be done next; Pamela Satran for undertaking the work of establishing an energetic community of writers in Montclair and for important comments on an early version of this work.

My debt to my family continues. As a memoirist, my parents and my grandparents, although deceased, are still with me, and I am grateful for their immense effort in educating me and for their stories, which I am trying to unlock the meaning of still. My sons, Jason DeSalvo and Justin DeSalvo, continue to be a source of pride and encouragement; my daughters-in-law, Deborah De-Salvo and Lynn DeSalvo, enrich my life daily. Deborah DeSalvo assisted with the research on Freud. My grandchildren, Steven Louis DeSalvo and Julia Frances May DeSalvo, are everyday reminders of the meaning of bliss. My husband, Ernie DeSalvo, edited a version of this manuscript and helped me discover what the next round of writing should look like; our life together, through its many transformations, provides the kind of stability every writer dreams of having.

My community of knitting friends at Stix-n-Stitches in Montclair has been a warm and supportive refuge after a writing day. I wish to thank Sheila Handelsman for creating a beautiful and welcoming space; Sunday Holm for encouragement about my writing and for teaching me new and complicated ways to practice the craft; and Debra Cottone for being a model of what daily attention to the creative process yields.

Through the years this book was in progress, many at Bloomsbury aided my work. I wish to thank Karen Rinaldi, Colin Dickerman, George Gibson, Amanda Katz, Kathy Belden, Katie Henderson, Greg Villepique, Natalie Slocum, Maureen Klier, Mike O'Connor, and Nancy Inglis, all of whom offered assistance at various stages.

Notes on the Sources

INTRODUCTION

Current moving statistics are from www.census.gov/population/www/pop-profile/geomob.html.

Effects of moving are described in Audrey McCollum, Nadia Jensen, and Stuart Copare, *Smart Moves: Your Guide Through the Emotional Maze of Relocation* (Manchester, NH: A. Smith and Kraus Book, 1996).

ONE

"A BALM TO CURE ALL ILLS": *Dream Houses*

Virginia Woolf's restiveness in Richmond, her love of house hunting, and her search for a London home are described in Virginia Woolf, *The Letters of Virginia Woolf*, vol. 2, 1920–1924, and vol. 3, 1923–1928, ed. Nigel Nicolson and Joanne Trautmann (London: Hogarth Press, 1976, 1977); and in *The Diary of Virginia Woolf*, vol. 1, 1915–1919, and vol. 2, 1920–1924, ed. Anne Olivier Bell (London: Hogarth Press, 1977, 1978); quotes are from these sources. Woolf describes Hyde Park as a cage in her memoir published in *Moments of Being*, ed. Jeanne Schulkind (New York: Harcourt Brace, 1976). Her dream of a house is in "Friendships Gallery," ed. Ellen Hawkes, *Twentieth Century Literature* 25 (Fall–Winter 1979); and in *A Passionate Apprentice*, ed. Mitchell Leaska (New York: Harcourt Brace, 1990). Woolf's buying Round House and Monk's House is described in *Diary* I.

I first became interested in Percy Bysshe Shelley's move to Italy, and in the unfortunate choice he made in Casa Magni, in reading Richard Holmes, *Footsteps* (New York: Penguin, 1985). Holmes's "Death and Destiny," *Guardian*, January 24, 2004, also describes this period. See also Claire Clairmont, *The Journals of Claire Clairmont, 1814–1827*, ed. Marion Kingston Stocking (Cambridge, MA: Harvard University Press, 1968); and Mary W. Shelley and Henry W. Harper, *Letters of Mary W. Shelley* (Boston: Bibliophile Society, 1918). All quotes from Shelley's letters are from Percy Bysshe Shelley, *Letters from Italy*, vol. 2, of the 1840 edition of *Essays, Letters from Abroad, Translations and Fragments, by Percy Bysshe Shelley*, ed. Mary Shelley, www.terpconnect.umn.edu/~djb/shelley/lettersfromitaly.html.

The novel I refer to by my friend Pamela Redmond Satran is *Suburbanistas* (New York: Downtown Press, 2006).

TWO
"A NEW AND BETTER WAY OF LIFE": *House Hunting*
Virginia and Leonard Woolf's quarrel upon house hunting is described in *The Diary of Virginia Woolf*, vol. 5, 1936–1941, ed. Anne Olivier Bell (London: Hogarth Press, 1984).

Daniel Gilbert's insights are found in his *Stumbling on Happiness* (New York: Alfred A. Knopf, 2006).

Lady Slane's house hunt, and her life thereafter, is the subject of Vita Sackville-West's *All Passion Spent* (Garden City, NY: Doubleday, Doran, 1931).

Vita Sackville-West's relationship to Harold Nicolson, their courtship and marriage, the search for the right home, and their refurbishing of Sissinghurst are described in their letters collected in Vita Sackville-West and Harold Nicolson, *Vita and Harold*, ed. Nigel Nicolson (New York: G. P. Putnam's Sons, 1992); Victoria Glendinning, *Vita* (New York: Alfred A. Knopf, 1983); and Harold Nicolson, *Diaries and Letters, 1930–1939*, ed. Nigel Nicolson (London: Collins, 1966). Vita's relationship with Violet is described in Nigel Nicolson, *Portrait of a Marriage* (New York: Atheneum, 1973). Vita describes Knole and her life there in *Knole and the Sackvilles* (London: Ernest Benn Ltd., 1973); a description appears in *The Edwardians* (New York: Doubleday, Doran, 1930). Leonard Woolf's description of Vita appears in *Downhill All the Way* (New York: Harcourt Brace Jovanovich, 1967).

Alain de Botton's insights about what satisfies—and what does not—in a home are found in *The Architecture of Happiness* (New York: Pantheon Books, 2006), and his insights about satisfaction are found, too, in *Status Anxiety* (New York: Pantheon Books, 2004).

THREE

"A HOME DISMANTLED": *Packing Up*

The Stephen King anecdote is taken from Motoko Rich, "Stephen King Explores Joy in Marriage, Grief in Loss," *New York Times*, October 4, 2006.

Information on Eugene O'Neill's childhood, the family's itinerant life, his mother's response to it, and their relationship to the themes in his work is based on Stephen A. Black, *Eugene O'Neill* (New Haven, CT: Yale University Press, 1999). See also John Orr, "Eugene O'Neill: The Life Remembered," in *Modern Critical Interpretations: Eugene O'Neill's Long Day's Journey into Night*, ed. Harold Bloom (New York: Chelsea House Publishers, 1987); and Eugene O'Neill, *Selected Letters of Eugene O'Neill*, ed. Travis Bogard and Jackson R. Bryer (New Haven: Yale University Press, 1988). All quotations from *Long Day's Journey into Night* are from the 1988 edition published by Yale University Press, New Haven, CT. Matthew Friedman's unpublished 2007 paper "The Idea of Home in Eugene O'Neill's *Long Day's Journey into Night*" references mentions of home in the drama.

All anecdotes about the Wodaabe are from Marion Van Offelen, *Nomads of the Niger*, with photographs by Carol Beckwith (New York: Abrams, n.d.).

Virginia Woolf describes the destruction of her London homes, her packing what remained, and their effect on her in *The Letters of Virginia Woolf*, vol. 5 and 6, ed. Nigel Nicolson and Joanne Trautmann (London: Hogarth Press, 1979, 1980); and in *The Diary of Virginia Woolf*, vol. 5, 1936–1941, ed. Anne Olivier Bell (London: Hogarth Press, 1984).

FOUR

"ADRIFT": *Life After Moving*

Eavan Boland describes her move to the suburbs in *Object Lessons* (New York: W. W. Norton and Company, 1955).

J. M. Coetzee describes his move to London in *Youth* (New York: Penguin Books, 2002).

Virginia Woolf describes her move from Hyde Park Gate most fully in *A Passionate Apprentice*, in *The Letters of Virginia Woolf*, vol. 1, 1888–1912, ed. Nigel Nicolson and Joanne Trautmann (London: Hogarth Press, 1975); and in "Old Bloomsbury," *Moments of Being*. For the impact of incest on Woolf, see my *Virginia Woolf: The Impact of Childhood Sexual Abuse on Her Life and Work* (Boston: Beacon Press, 1989).

FIVE

"A SPACE FOR THE PSYCHE'S HINTERLAND":
Homemaking

Mark Doty's comment on blossoming is in *Dog Years* (New York: HarperCollins, 2007).

Carl Jung's building is described most fully in his memoir *Memories, Dreams, Reflections*, ed. Aniela Jaffe, trans. Richard Winston and Clara Winston (New York: Vintage, 1963). Deirdre Bair, *Jung* (New York: Little, Brown, 2003) contextualizes this act.

Marguerite Duras's purchase of the house at Neauphle-le-Château and its effect on her life and work is described in *Writing*, trans. Mark Polizzotti (Cambridge, MA: Lumen Editions, 1993). The loss of her childhood home is described in many of Duras's novels, most notably *The Sea Wall*, trans. Herma Briffault (New York: Harper and Row, 1986). Her mother's violence is described in *The North China Lover*, trans. Leigh Hafrey (New York: New Press, 1992). Alain Vircondelet, *Duras*, trans. Thomas Buckley (Normal, IL: Dalkey Archive Press, 1994), describes the works she wrote here and the shift in her style.

Pierre Bonnard's house at Le Cannet and the shift in his work are described in Nicholas Watkins, *Bonnard* (New York: Phaidon Press, 1994). Bonnard's changes to the house and his aesthetic are described in Michel Terrasse, *Bonnard at Le Cannet* (London: Thames and Hudson, 1988). Bonnard's and Henri Matisse's correspondence is found in Pierre Bonnard and Henri Matisse, *Bonnard/Matisse*, trans. Richard Howard (New York: Harry N. Abrams, 1991). Also useful were Raymond Cogniat, *Bonnard* (New York: Crown, 1979); Julius Muriel, "Pierre Bonnard at the Villa Le Bosquet," *Contemporary Review*, August 1994; John Rewald, *Pierre Bonnard* (New York: Museum of Modern Art, 1948); and James Thrall Soby, James Elliott, and Monroe Wheeler, *Bonnard and His Environment* (Garden City, NY: Doubleday, 1964), where his inclusion in the Nabis is described.

SIX

"DISPLACED": *Exiles, Refugees, Wanderers*
Elizabeth Bishop's feeling displaced, her sense of geography, all the places she lived in, and the moves she made are described in Brett C. Millier, *Elizabeth Bishop* (Berkeley: University of California Press, 1993)—Millier cites many of Bishop's poems and letters on this theme—and in Elizabeth Spires, "The Art of Poetry," an interview with Elizabeth Bishop, *Paris Review Interviews*, 1 (New York: Picador, 2006). The letter describing her as the loneliest person who ever lived is found in Bishop, *One Art*, ed. Robert Giroux (New York: Farrar, Straus and Giroux, 1994); other letters in this volume describe Bishop's childhood in Great Village, her passion for travel, her life in Key West, and her life with Lota in Brazil. Bishop's mother's illness is described in "In the Village," *The Collected Prose* (New York: Farrar, Straus and Giroux, 1995). Bishop's

poems appear in *The Complete Poems* (New York: Farrar, Straus and Giroux, 1983). Bishop's asthma is described in her letters and in Marilyn May Lombardi, "The Closet of Breath," *Twentieth Century Literature* 38:2 (Summer 1992). A fictionalized treatment of her relationship with Lota is described in Carmen L. Oliveira, *Rare and Commonplace Flowers*, trans. Neil K. Besner (New Brunswick, NJ: Rutgers University Press, 2002).

Freud's hearing about the invasion of the Nazis and the events thereafter are chronicled in Ernest Jones, *The Life and Work of Sigmund Freud* (New York: Basic Books, 1961, abridged edition); Peter Gay, *Freud* (New York: W. W. Norton, 2006); and Diana Fuss, *The Sense of an Interior* (New York: Routledge, 2004). His leaving Vienna is described in Gay, Jones, and H[ilda]. D[oolittle]., *Tribute to Freud* (Oxford: Carcanet Press, 1971). Moving the artifacts is described in Fuss and in Janine Burke, *The Sphinx on the Table* (New York: Walker and Company, 2006). The collection and its history is detailed in Burke and also described by Fuss and H. D. Clare Cooper Marcus in *House as a Mirror of Self* (Berkeley, CA: Conari Press, 1995) describes the importance of moving beloved objects. Freud's interior decorating is described in Burke and Gay. The Woolfs' meeting with Freud is described in Leonard Woolf, *Downhill All the Way* (New York: Harcourt Brace Jovanovich, 1967); and in Virginia Woolf, *The Diary of Virginia Woolf*, vol. 5, 1936–1941, ed. Anne Olivier Bell (London: Hogarth Press, 1984); a description of the study at the time is provided in Janine Burke, "Freud's Affair with Pagan Splendor," *The Age*, September 30, 2006, www.theage.com.au/news/books/sigmunds-great-obsession/2006/09/28/1159337277484.html. Descriptions of Freud's death are in the biographies cited above and in H. D.

Placing D. H. Lawrence's position as an outsider as a central feature of his life is developed in John Worthen, *D. H. Lawrence* (New York: Counterpoint, 2005). My tally of Lawrence's abodes and the descriptions of his homes, his travels, and the composition of his work comes from Worthen's descriptions and from *The Letters of D. H. Lawrence*, vol. 1, September 1901–May 1913, ed. James T. Boulton; vol. 2, June 1913–October 1916, ed. George J. Zytaruk, James T. Boulton, and Andrew Robertson; vol. 3, October 1916–June 1921, ed. James T. Boulton and Andrew Robertson; vol. 4, June 1921–March 1924, ed. Warren Roberts, James T. Boulton, and Elizabeth Mansfield; vol. 5, March 1924–March 1927, ed. James T. Boulton and Lindeth Vasey (Cambridge: Cambridge University Press, 1979, 1981, 1984, 1987, 1989). Lawrence's early life is chronicled in Worthen, *Lawrence* (Cambridge: Cambridge University Press, 1991). The marriage to Frieda is described in Worthen and in Brenda Maddox, *D. H. Lawrence* (New York: Simon and Schuster, 1994). The trip to Sardinia, describing Lawrence's analysis of his need to move on, is found in *Sea and Sardinia* (Garden City, NY: Doubleday and Company, 1954). Paulo's story is told in *Twilight in Italy* (Doylestown, PA: Wildside Press, 1916). Lawrence's love of Cornwall, he and Frieda's treatment in Cornwall, their expulsion, the banning of *The Rainbow,* and his ideas on property ownership are fully described in Lawrence's letters from the time. Their life in Ceylon and Australia is described in Worthen.

SEVEN

"A DOOR, OPENING": *Changing Lives*
Mark Doty's nomadic childhood and his mother's dream are recounted in his memoir *Firebird* (New York: Perennial, 2000). Doty's need for permanence but the allure of change is described

in *Still Life with Oysters and Lemon* (Boston: Beacon, 2001). His and Wally's early life together in Boston, Doty's return visits, his meeting Wally, his early life in New York, their refurbishing the house in Vermont, their life in Provincetown, and Wally's illness and death are described in *Heaven's Coast* (New York: HarperCollins, 1996). Their life in Vermont, buying the cabin, and renting the house on the tip of the Cape are recorded in *Dog Years* (New York: HarperCollins, 2007). The move to Fire Island is described in Beth Greenfield, "Trading One Beach Retreat for Another," *New York Times*, June 8, 2007.

Sara Jenkins's description of her discomfort in a house and how she resolves it are described in her *This Side of Nirvana* (Gloucester, MA: Fair Winds Press, 2001).

Henry Miller's first trip to Paris with June and his relationship with her are described in *My Life and Times* (New York: Playboy Press, n.d.); and Mary V. Dearborn, *Henry Miller* (New York: Simon and Schuster, 1991). The bicycle trip is also described in *Tropic of Cancer* (New York: Grove Press, 1961). Miller's second trip to Paris, his life there, his becoming a writer, and his leaving a place for good are described in his *Cancer, My Life and Times, Letters to Emil*, ed. George Wickes (New York: New Directions, 1989); and in Dearborn, *Henry Miller* (New York: Simon and Schuster, 1991); Jay Martin, *Always Merry and Bright* (Santa Barbara, CA: Capra Press, 1978); Miller, *Quiet Days in Clichy* (New York: Grove Press, 1956); Alfred Perlès, *My Friend Henry Miller* (New York: John Day, 1956); and Robert Snyder, *This Is Henry Miller from Brooklyn* (Los Angeles: Nash Publishing, 1974). His romance with Anaïs Nin is described in their letters collected in *A Literary Passion*, ed. Gunther Stuhlmann (New York: Harcourt Brace Jovanovich, 1987).

EIGHT

MOVING ON

Moving's ancient history is described in Nicholas Wade, *Before the Dawn* (New York: Penguin Press, 2006); Spencer Wells, *The Journey of Man* (New York: Random House, 2002); Wells's *The Journey of Man* (DVD video, PBS, 2003); and in Rory Stewart, *The Places in Between* (New York: Harcourt, 2004). Wells's work prompted me to join the National Geographic Genographic Project and to have my DNA tested; my ancestresses' migrations are described in the results; see http://nationalgeographic.com/geno graphic.

For conditions in Puglia causing my grandfather's emigration, see Frank M. Snowden, *Violence and the Great Estates in the South of Italy: Apulia, 1900–1922* (Cambridge: Cambridge University Press, 2004).

Pauline Boss's *Ambiguous Loss* (Cambridge, MA: Harvard University Press, 1999) is essential reading for determining the impact of belonging to an émigré family.

The story of the relationship between Korean immigrants and the people from Guatemala in Palisades Park was reported by Elizabeth Llorente in "A Tale of Two Cultures: A Pharmacist Learns to Reach Across the Divide," *Bergen Record*, August 23, 1998; and in "A Tale of Two Cultures: Immigrants' Alliance, Palisades Park Koreans Lend Hand to Guatemalans," *Bergen Record*, December 7, 1998.

AFTERWORD

Portions of Henry Miller's notebooks are reproduced in his *My Life and Times* (New York: Playboy Press, n.d.).

Virginia Woolf's "Haunted House" appears in *A Haunted House and Other Stories* (New York: Harcourt, Brace and World, 1949). Her description of returning to Talland House appears in *A Passionate Apprentice*, ed. Mitchell Leaska (New York: Harcourt Brace, 1990).

Louise DeSalvo is a writer, professor, lecturer, and scholar who lives in New Jersey. She is currently the Jenny Hunter Endowed Scholar for Literature and Creative Writing at Hunter College and has recently been awarded a Premio Letterario Giuseppe Acerbi Prize. Her many books include the memoirs *Crazy in the Kitchen, Vertigo, Breathless,* and *Adultery;* the acclaimed biography *Virginia Woolf: The Impact of Childhood Sexual Abuse on Her Life and Work;* and *Writing as a Way of Healing.* She recently moved.